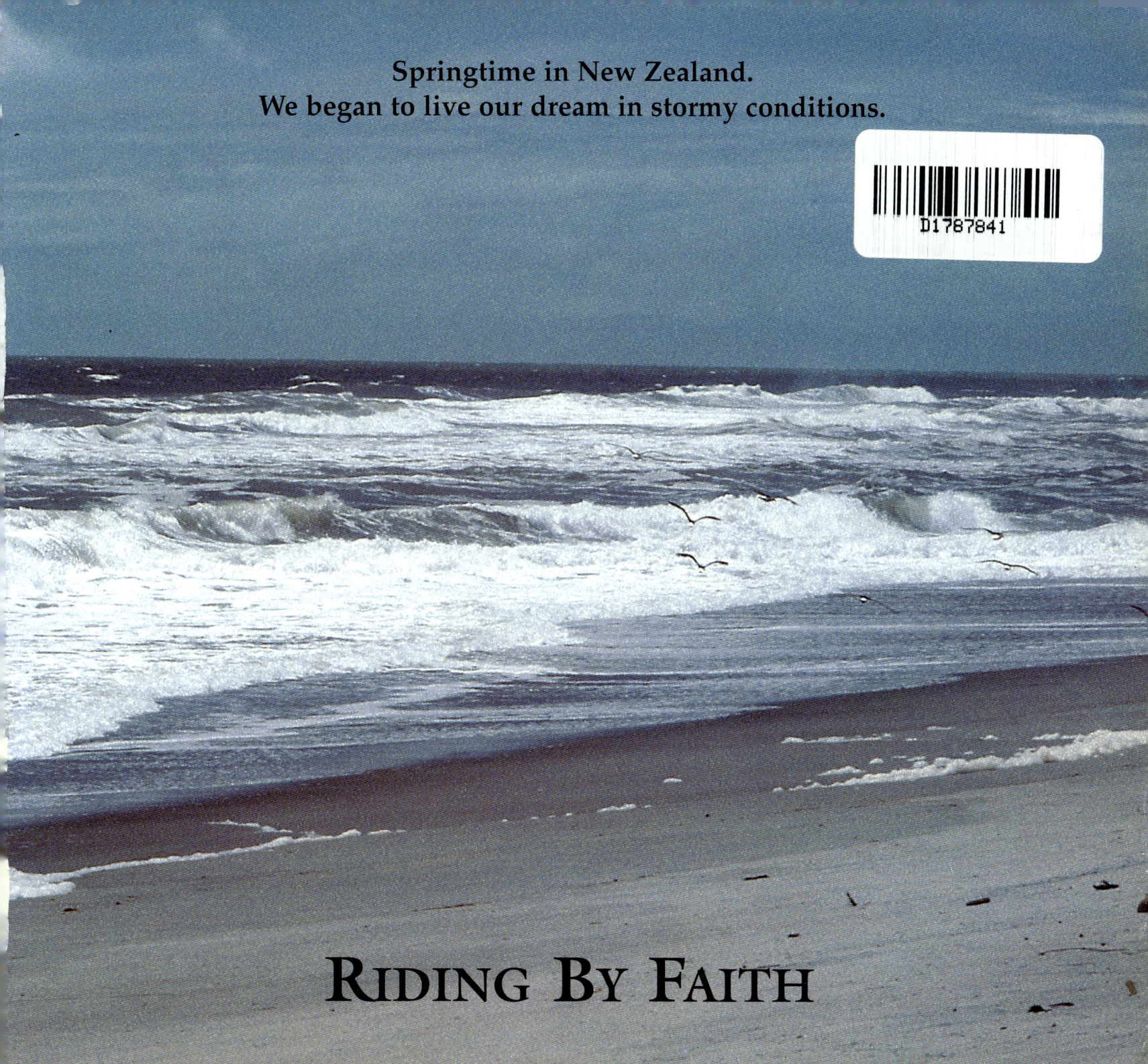

THANKS TO   Shan Palmes for all your help and encouragement with this book
Shona Barr, Mac Barribal, Bob and Lesley Somers
Ali for dreaming and riding with me
And to all the hospitable New Zealanders who helped us on our way
God bless you all

TEXT AND PHOTOGRAPHS © Tracey Elliot-Reep 2003
Designed and published by Tracey Elliot-Reep
Shilstone Rocks, Widecombe-in-the-Moor,
Devon, TQ13 7TF, England
www.traceyelliotreep.com

Printed in England by Alpine Press
Station Road, Kings Langley,
Hertfordshire
WD4 8LF
ISBN 0 9538231-1-3 Paperback

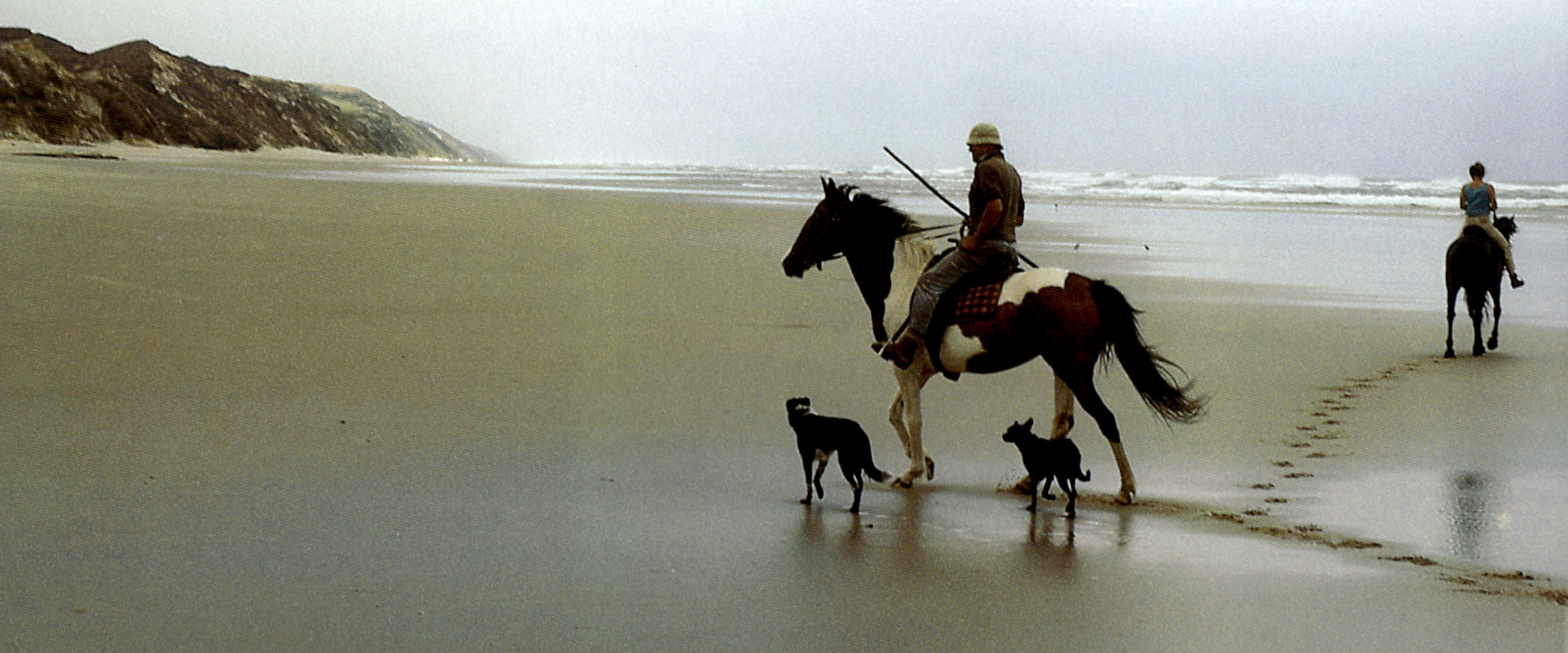

All Scripture references are from the New King James Bible (NKJ) Copyright © 1979, 1980, 1982, 1991, by Thomas Nelson, Inc. Unless otherwise indicated. Versions used in Riding by Faith; New International Version (NIV) The Amplified Bible (Amp) The Living Bible (TLB) The Good News Bible (GNB) The Message (TM) New Living Translation (NLT) Free Translation (FT)
All rights reserved. No part of this publication may be reproduced, stored in a retrieval system, or transmitted, in any form or by any means, electronic, mechanical, photocopying, recording or otherwise, without prior permission in writing of the publisher.

FOREWORD

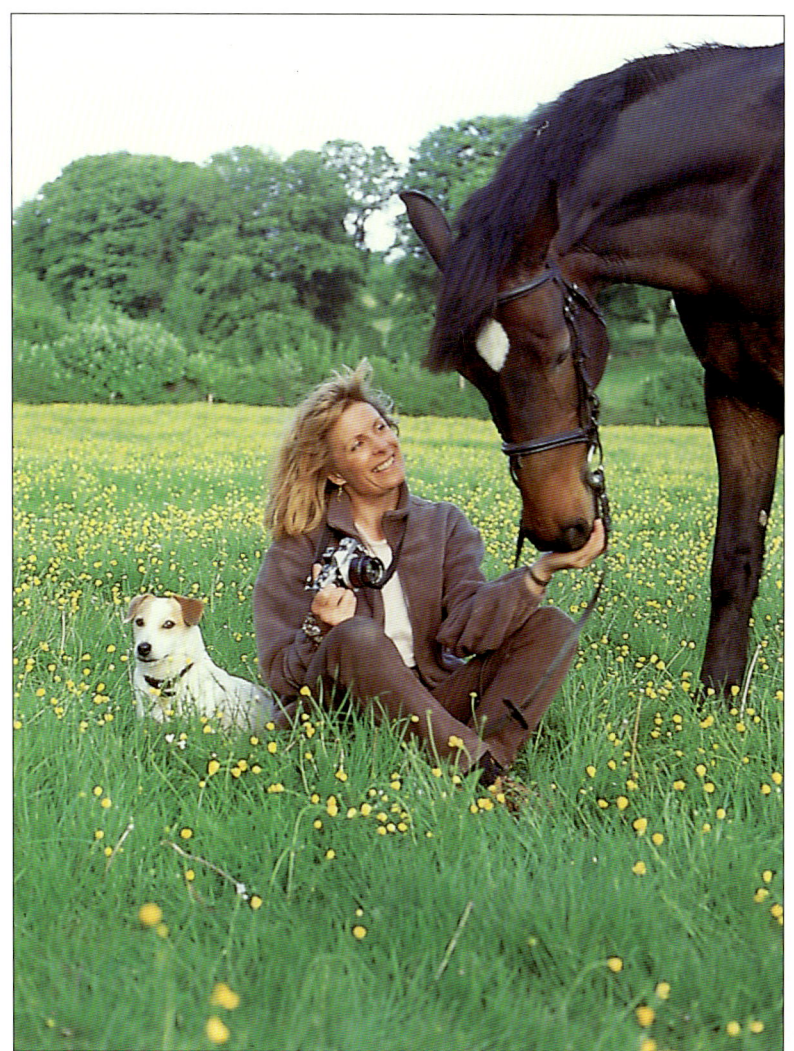

Riding by Faith Through New Zealand will beautifully show you in photos and words an adventure with God lived by Tracey and her friend Ali. You will be amazed as you get to know two young women who live life to the fullest.

A gutsy woman! That describes Tracey Elliot-Reep. Full of adventure and exploits, full of faith in her God. She is a dreamer who puts action to her dreams with hard work. Tracey is generous with her life, letting the Light in her life shine for all to see. By living this way, she desires that others will be prompted to open up to God, our generous Father in heaven.

It's only forever!

Dave and Bonnie Duell

Dave and Bonnie Duell
Faith Ministries International Network
Denver, Colorado USA

Contents

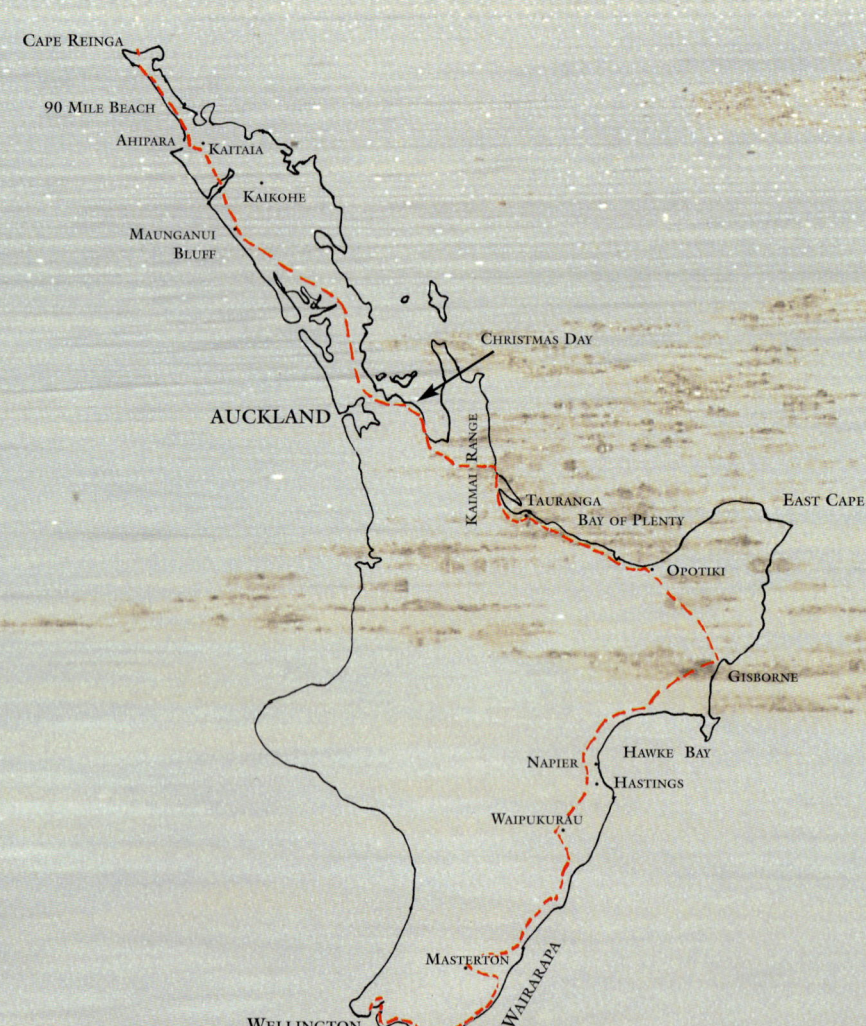

The North Island

Foreword
Introduction

2. The Start
3. 90 Mile Beach
4. Ahipara
5. Maunganui Bluff
6. Auckland
7. 3 Lunches!
8. Christmas Day
9. 3 Horses
10. Lost and Found
11. No hoof no horse
12. An Angel in disguise!
13. Cyclone
14. Rest and Respite
15. Sheepskins
16. Waioeka Gorge
17. Hawke's Bay
18. Honey
19. Losing things
20. Factor 15!
21. Wellington
22. Lost in the Capital
23. Waiting on the Quay
24. Cook Strait

The South Island

25. The South Island
26. Molesworth
27. Jollies Pass
28. Hanmer Springs
29. Harper Pass
30. Cliff Edge
31. Digger's Grave
32. The Otira
33. Easter Day!
34. Christchurch
35. Coleridge Saddle
36. The High Country
37. The Rangitata
38. Clayton Station
39. The Mackenzie Country
40. Queenstown
41. Monty's Fall
42. Bluff

Epilogue

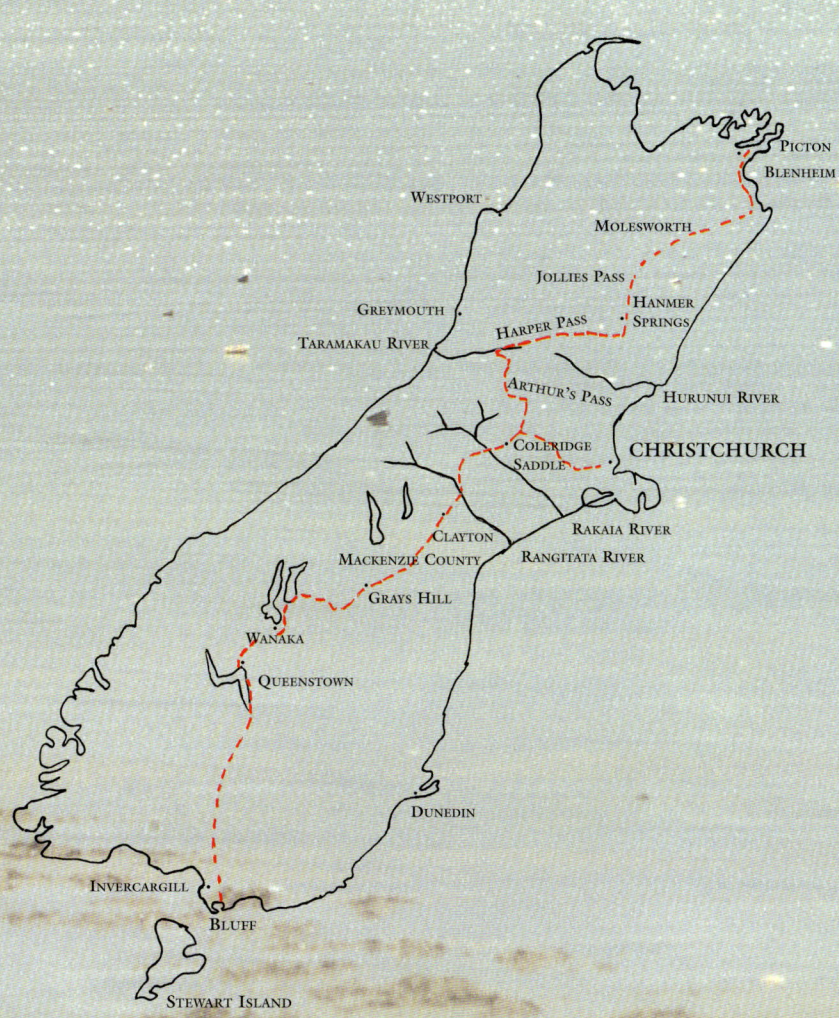

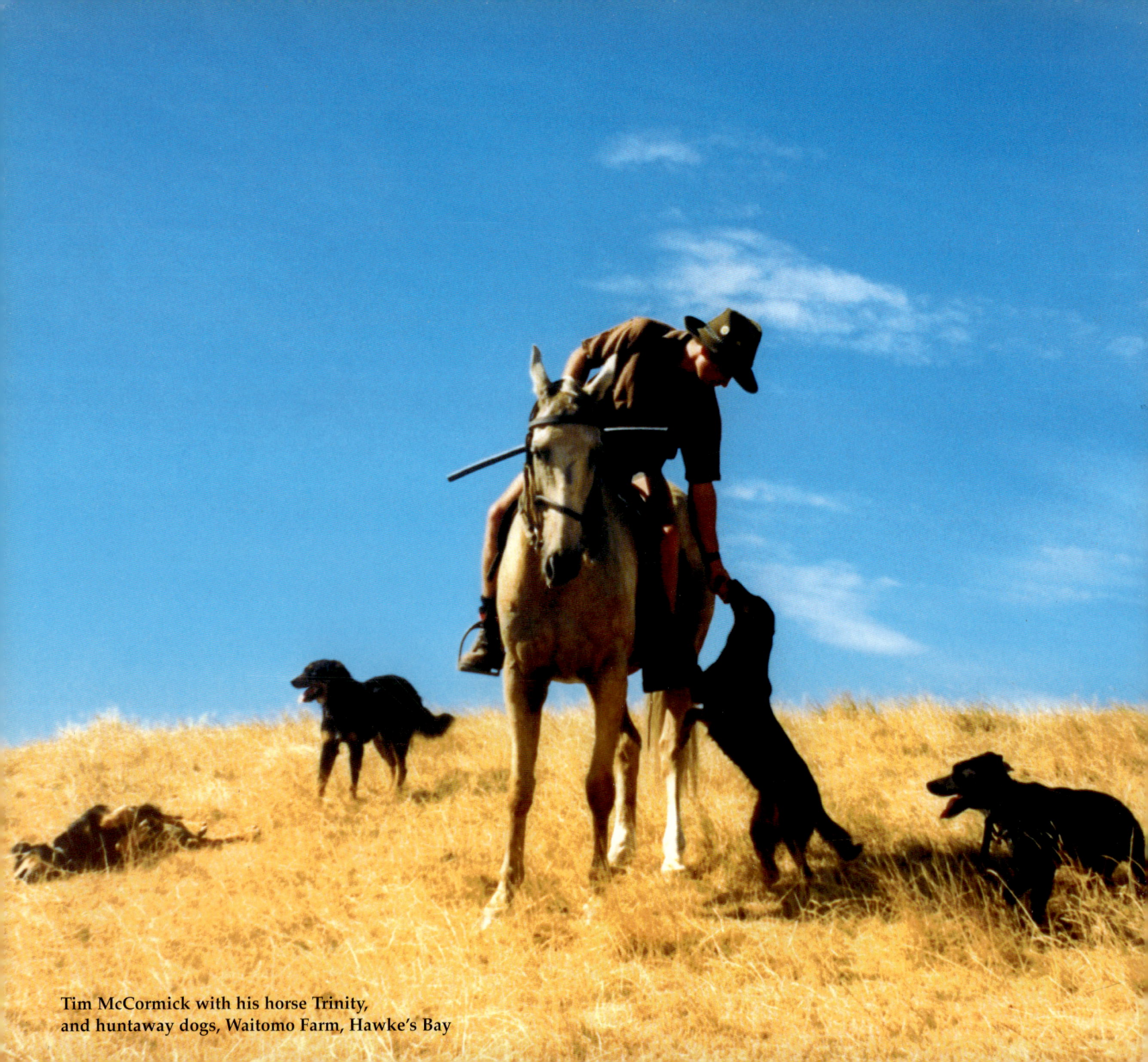

Tim McCormick with his horse Trinity, and huntaway dogs, Waitomo Farm, Hawke's Bay

INTRODUCTION

I grew up with horses on a Dartmoor farm in South West England. Following school I did an art and design course, and then applied to do a fine art degree. My application was turned down, so instead, along with my sketchbook I joined a travelling circus. There I saved just enough for a ticket to Israel where I worked on a Kibbutz overlooking the Sea of Galilee.

After a few months milking cows and working in a silver workshop, I hitch hiked to Jerusalem and it was overlooking the city glowing golden in the evening sunlight, on Israel's Independence Day, that I invited Jesus into my life.

A year later, I was offered a job teaching horse riding, English style, on a children's summer camp in Michigan, U.S.A. I asked God to bring another Christian into the camp and I met Ali Gough who had grown up in north-east Scotland, was studying for a degree in Communication Studies and had also been praying the same prayer! We were both 20 years old, loved God, horses and adventure!

THE IDEA   *Do not despise this small beginning.* Zechariah 4:10 TLB

Five years later, crouched forward in my saddle, my face buried in my horse's flying mane, we raced neck and neck across Dartmoor. After a short fast sprint our mounts began to ease their pace. We came to a standstill on the crest of Hamel down Hill, overlooking the small village of Widecombe-in-the-Moor with its houses clustered around the tall, sixteenth century church tower.

Exhilarated and slightly breathless, I turned to Ali, astride a dark bay mare glistening with sweat and impulsively suggested,

"How about riding up to the North Coast of Devon, it's only about a hundred miles?" She nodded in agreement.

"Or, how about riding," I paused as my imagination stretched my ambition, "Up the west coast of Britain?"

"Sure!" came her reply. Caught in a spiral of ambitious journeys, out of my mouth came,

"Or how about riding across New Zealand?"

"Why not!" she said with a big smile and a chuckle.

To be honest, I don't even know if either of us knew what New Zealand actually looked like! After riding home to look at my old school atlas, and discovering that New Zealand was long and narrow we changed the across to the length. Nine months later we arrived in New Zealand with only £60 (NZ$180) between us.

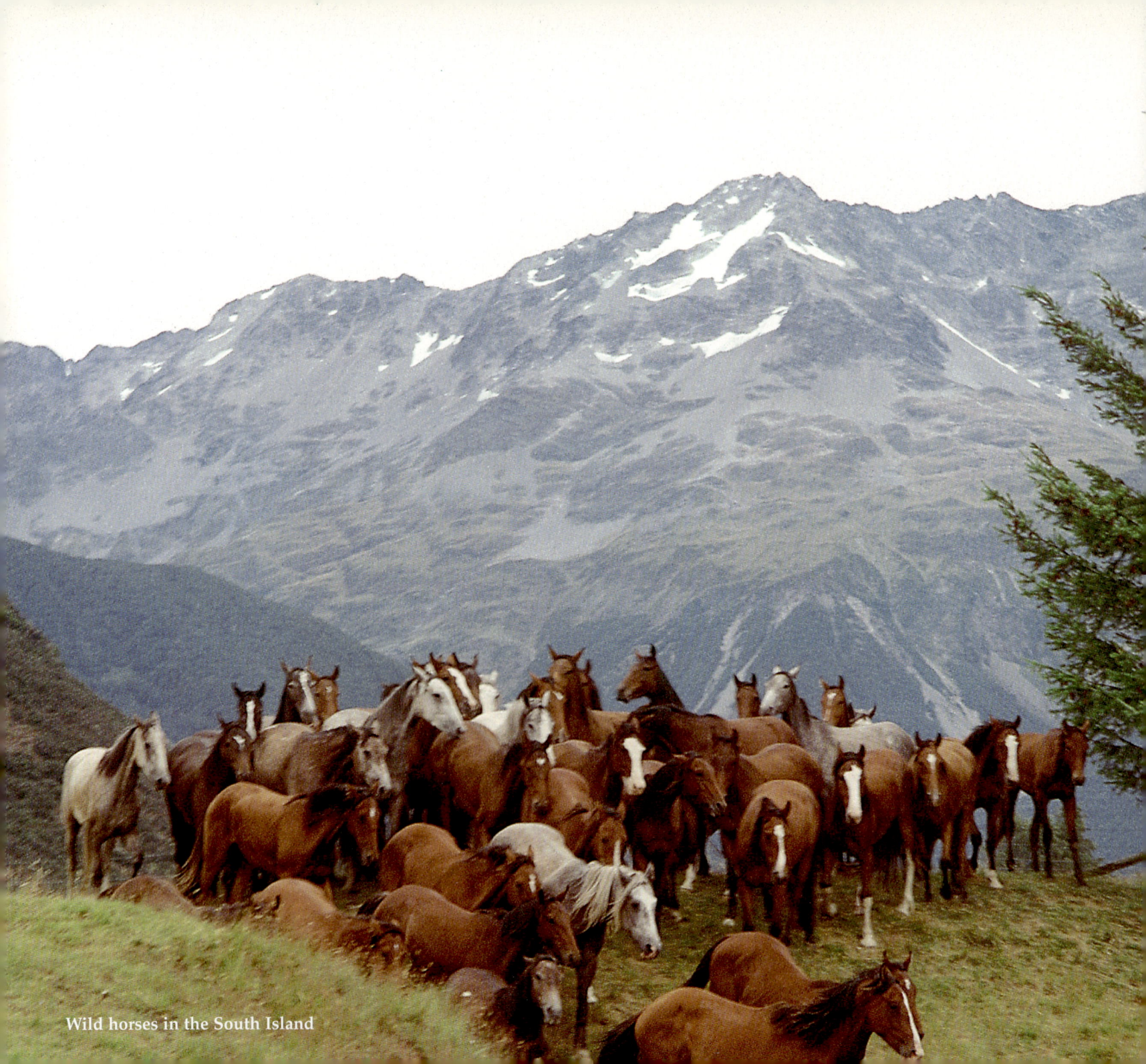
Wild horses in the South Island

ARRIVAL   *For a dream comes through much business and painful effort.* Ecclesiastes 5:3 Amp

£60 didn't last long and some people laughed at the two pommie sheilas' dream! But we knew all things were possible with God.

Our first job was in Hawke's Bay picking apples. We camped in the orchard amongst the trees and waited until all the rest of the picking gang had gone home before taking a shower. We took turns, balanced on a gang plank of wood laid across a sea of mud, bracing ourselves while the other turned on the stop cock and a sudden burst of icy water poured out of a large pipeline above us. After several weeks we were rained out of our tent and slept with a surging generator in the pack shed. Sleepless nights compelled us to upgrade our accommodation to a wool shed shared with mice which startled us awake as they ran across us in the night! Often the whole shed stank and shook with hundreds of bleating, shuffling sheep. But we were thankful for a sturdy roof over our heads, especially when a devastating cyclone tore through northern Hawke's Bay.

Saving hard to buy horses, working every daylight hour, we were up before dawn cycling ten miles to pick fruit until dusk. Then, exhausted, shoulder-to-shoulder we cycled back in the dark with only the beam of one head light back to our shared accommodation.

Our next job was grading Kiwi fruit in a pack shed in The Bay of Plenty where I dreamt away the monotony, imagining us riding across New Zealand. After the Kiwi fruit season we still needed more finances to buy horses and equipment for our expedition. Ali suggested we got ski jobs.

"But Ali, I can't ski!" I reminded her.   "I have never skied in my life!"

"Oh, you'll love it!" she replied casually. So we prayed for ski jobs and got some in a South Island resort overlooking the beautiful Ohau lake where we waited on tables all evening and skied all day ! I very soon learned!

VISAS   *Do not, therefore fling away your fearless confidence.* Hebrews 10:35 Amp

While waiting on tables and skiing at Ohau, our New Zealand six month visas expired, so we caught a lift to Christchurch to get them renewed for another nine months.

"No way!" came the indignant reply to our polite request. Our impression that all New Zealanders were laid back was suddenly shattered. "Six months is the maximum extension allowed and due to your limited funds I can only grant you two more months."

"Only two more months!" We groaned as his words loaded with disappointment hit us hard. The dream which we had been working towards for six months began to crumble.

"Your two month extension will be ready to collect in a couple of days," he stated indifferently.

"I can't believe it Ali!" I sighed as we left the office, "All that hard slog and saving for nothing."

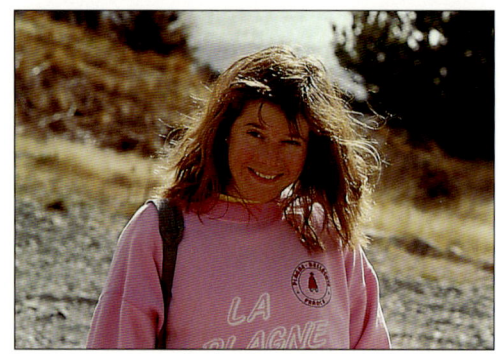

Ali at Lake Ohau

Favour   *You surround them with your favour as with a shield.* Psalm 5:12 NIV

After two days we returned to pick up our two months extensions. There was a different official who inquired as we approached the counter;
  "Why did you apply for a nine month extension? It's government policy that visitors can't stay more than a year." We explained that we needed that time to ride the whole length of New Zealand.
  "Excuse me, just a minute," he said disappearing into a back room. When he reappeared he handed us our passports saying with a smile on his face,
  "Have a nice trip!" Fumbling to open them at the right page we found that stamped on the page was a nine month extension!
  "Thank you so much!" we exclaimed. Elated, clutching our passports we skipped out of the office thanking God for his great faithfulness and favour.

Old Pack Saddle   *Trust in the Lord with all your heart and do not lean on your own understanding; in all your ways acknowledge Him, and He will direct your path.* Proverbs 3:5,6 NKJ

Three of our nine months had already slipped away and we still had no horses, supplies or equipment apart from one old borrowed pack-saddle. Although we had worked hard for nine months, we still only had limited funds, not enough to buy the horses, equipment and supplies needed for the ride. It looked like this expedition just wasn't going to happen! Then Ali suggested we fund raise for charity on our trek.

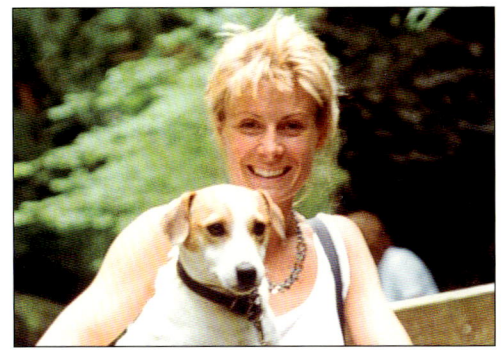
Tracey and Sam

Equipment   *My God will meet all your needs.* Philippians 4:19 NIV

We made the decision to raise money for Tearfund (The Evangelical Alliance Relief Fund), to help the recent Bangladesh flood victims. The next day we had a phone call from the equestrian magazine *Hoofprints* which had heard of our intended expedition and were interested in featuring our ride in their monthly magazine.

Their proposal was to supply us with all the equipment we needed, through donations from their advertisers. In return we would phone in reports of our progress and send in photos along the way. Our list of necessary items was extensive!

Looking for Horses   *We should make plans - counting on God to direct us.* Proverbs 16:9 TLB

Now we were well equipped, but still no horses, so we travelled north and started our search. After a week of looking at unsuitable horses with a Maori meat-man escorting us, we found ourselves at Kaikohe cattle market. Here we met Ken Lewis, an old drover hobbling on his wooden leg. He invited us further north to his homestead at Kaitaia so we loaded our new equipment and our old borrowed pack-saddle into his open topped cattle truck. We climbed in with half a dozen huntaway dogs and half a carcass of beef, swarming with flies. As the truck sped off along the gravel road, leaving behind most of the flies the dust billowed in and engulfed us and all our new equipment - and I wondered if we had made the right decision!

1
OUR HORSES

Trust in the living God, who gives us richly all things to enjoy 1 Timothy 6:17 NKJ

The evening shadows stretched out as the truck bumped up the rough track towards Ken's homestead. At the top, a young, inquisitive looking 15 hand, chestnut gelding with a white blaze, leant over a wire fence to greet us. This was Monty who was destined to become our mischievous and endearing pack-horse. He had never worn a pack before and disliked being led, preferring to be independent, sometimes hanging back for a mouthful of grass or trotting on ahead, introducing himself to strangers and invading any picnics which happened on the way! He habitually rolled on our carefully balanced packs so our metal cups became chipped ovals and our powdered milk exploded throughout the entire pack!

Next, we were introduced to Queenie, a nervous young dun-coloured mare who cavorted and snorted around us with her head held high and tail flying out behind her.

Our third horse was Nelson, a 16 hand dark bay gelding with one wall eye. He was really too big to keep in good condition for such an expedition, but it was love at first sight as he trotted over the crest of the hill towards us at the sound of his name.

"We'll never be able to part with him!" I exclaimed as I stroked his conker-coloured neck.

"But Trace, we haven't even bought him yet!" Ali laughed. After persuading his owner to sell him, Nelson with his high head carriage and long swinging stride became our gallant leader.

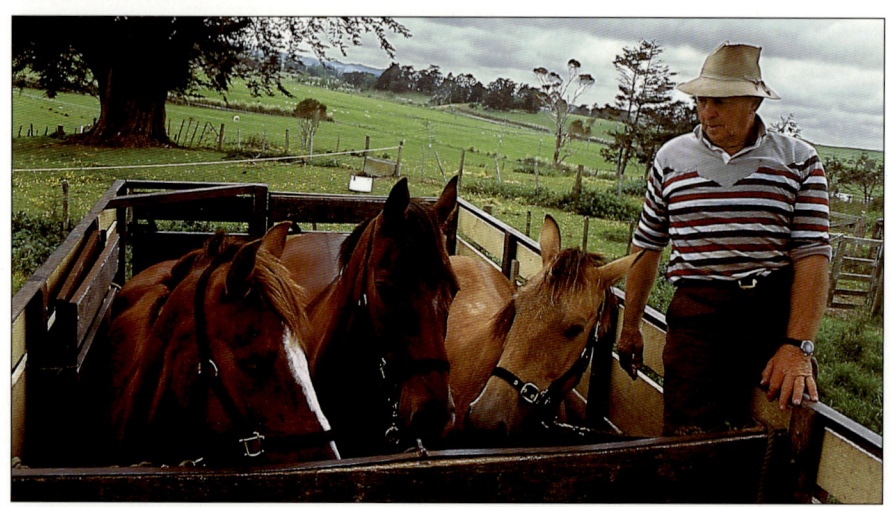

Monty, Nelson and Queenie with Ken Lewis in his convertible

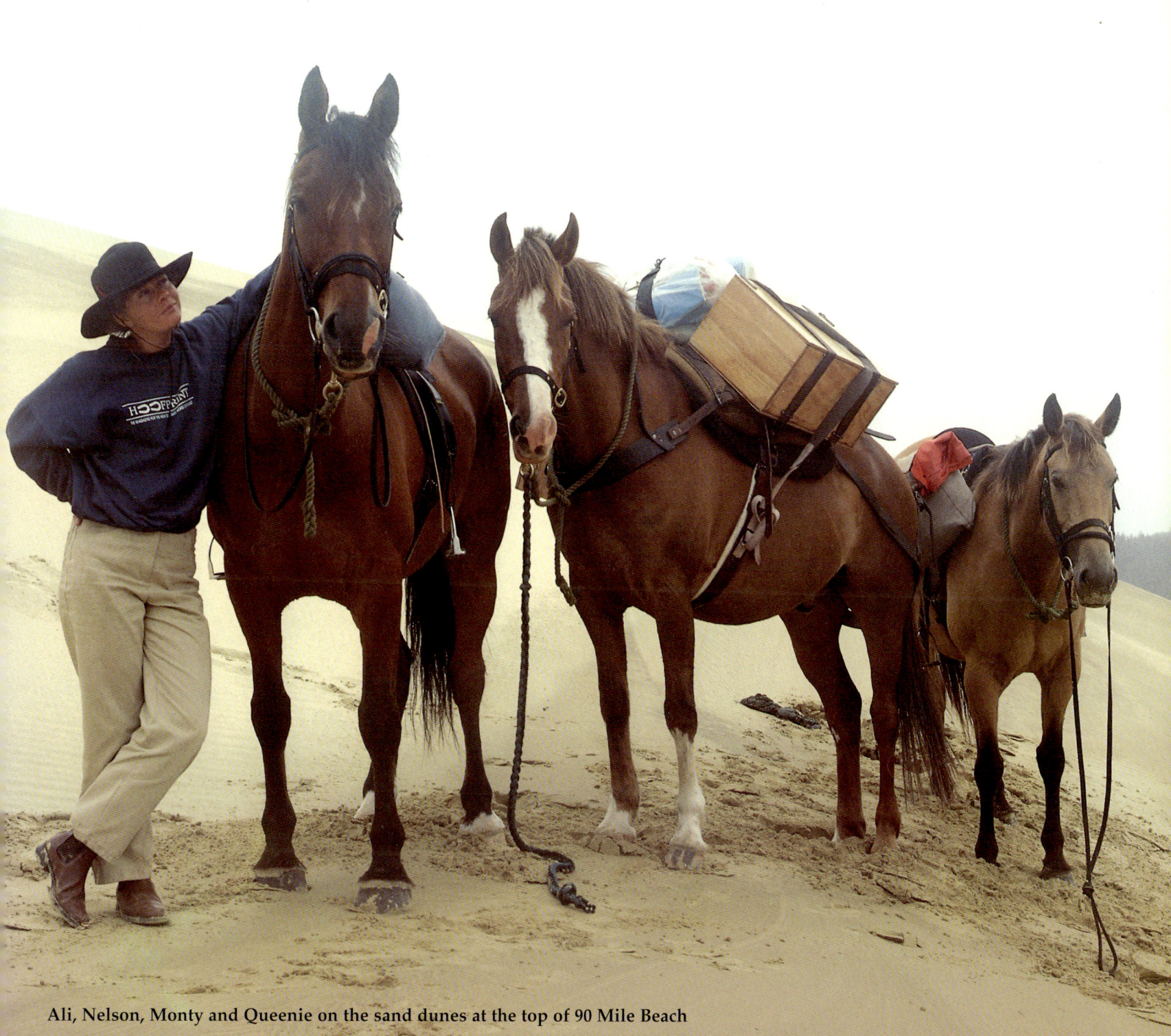

Ali, Nelson, Monty and Queenie on the sand dunes at the top of 90 Mile Beach

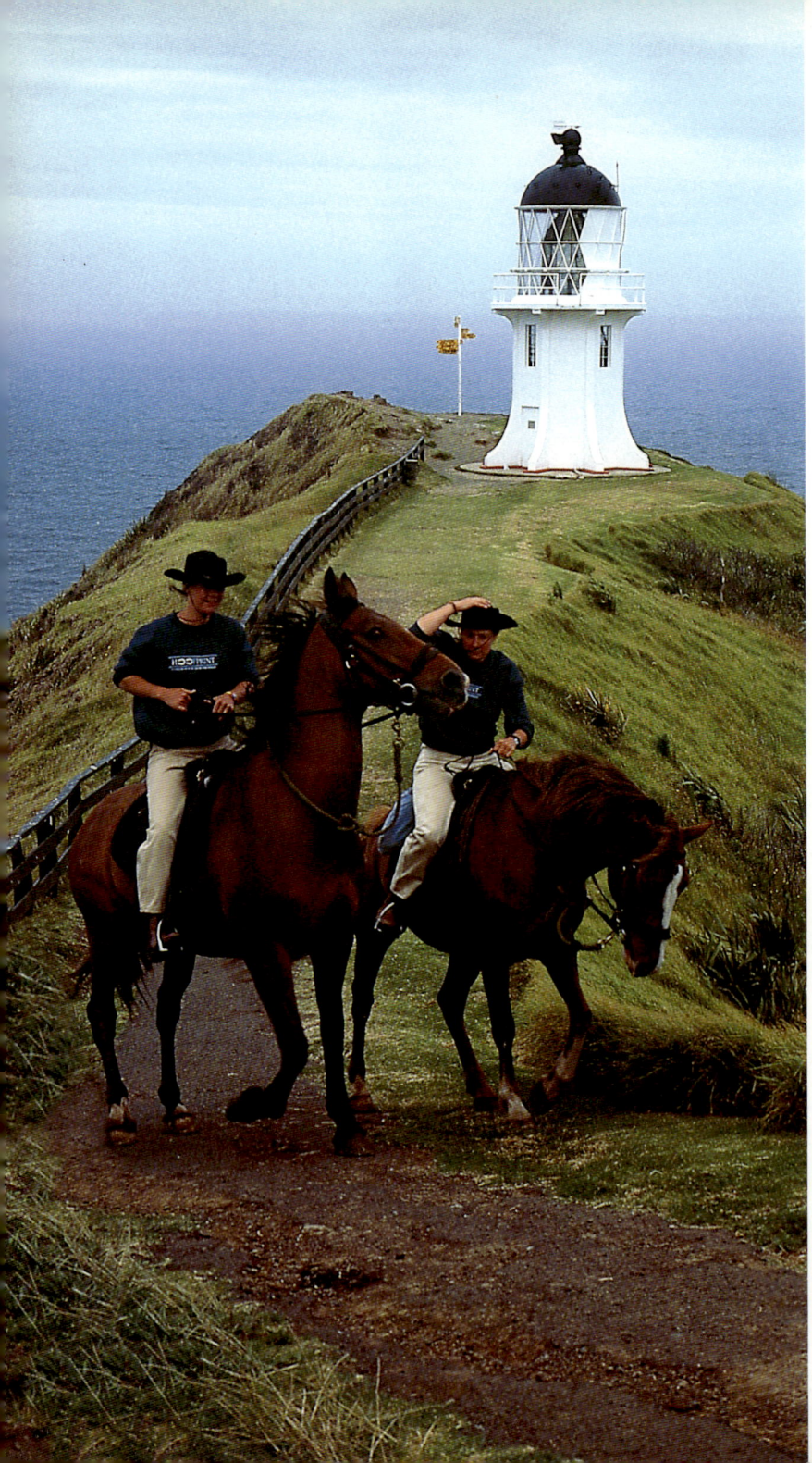

2
THE START

My heart rejoices in the Lord
1 Samuel 2:1 NKJ

On a windy November day, we set off from Cape Reinga, the most northerly point of New Zealand where the Tasman Sea butts up against the Pacific Ocean.

As we rode away from the solitary lighthouse the wind buffeted us on every flank, tousled our horses' manes and snatched at our hats but nothing could stop our hearts overflowing with exhilaration and thankfulness. At long last, we had begun to live our dream!

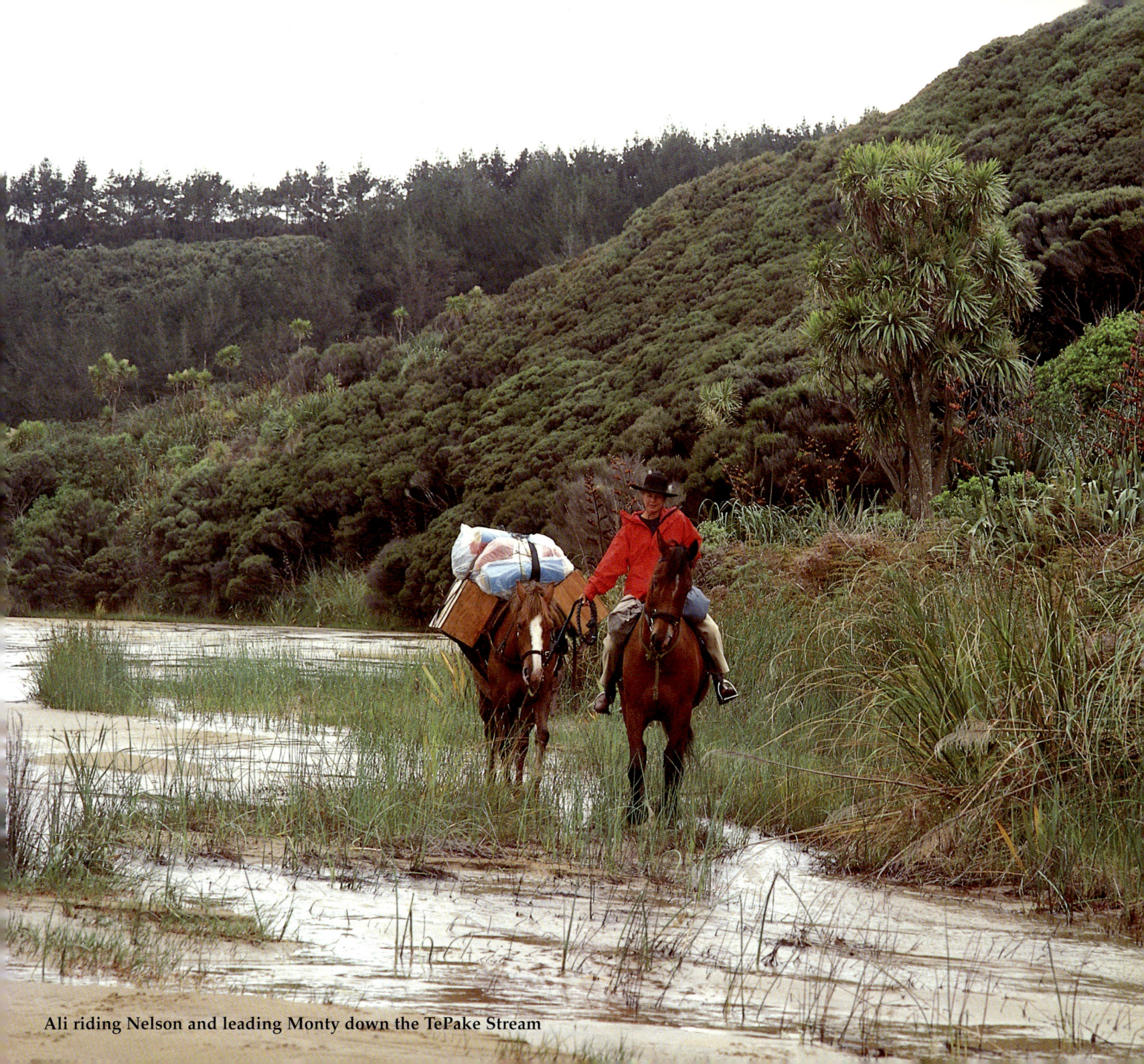
Ali riding Nelson and leading Monty down the TePake Stream

3
90 Mile Beach

The righteous cry out, and the Lord hears, and delivers them out of all their troubles.
Psalm 34:17 NKJ

We left hoof prints in the deep sand as we clambered up monstrous dunes onto a high windswept desert and then descended on to 90 Mile beach stretching southward. That was after some initial disagreement, when Monty refused to follow on the lead rein across the sand and pulled Ali backwards off Nelson!

Abel Tasman, the first European to discover New Zealand in 1643, had called this barren stretch of sand the Desert Coast. Today, huge areas of radiator pine trees line extensive sections of the beach. (New Zealand has the fastest growing trees in the world mainly due to its climate).

Our horses were edgy, never having seen the sea before and when they felt the water lapping at their legs and the shifting sand beneath their hooves, they nervously shied away from the incoming white-capped waves. Accompanied only by gliding seagulls we continued south, along the far-stretching beach. Intending to have a short first day we turned our horses inland through a forest to find fresh water and a grassy paddock. For the next eight hours we were trapped in the forest, following tracks leading to nowhere.

Exhausted, the grassy verge looked so inviting to collapse into, but the reality drove us on. If we lost our horses in the forest overnight we would never find them again. So, as if sleep walking, we plodded on following yet another track, desperately hoping it would lead to somewhere.

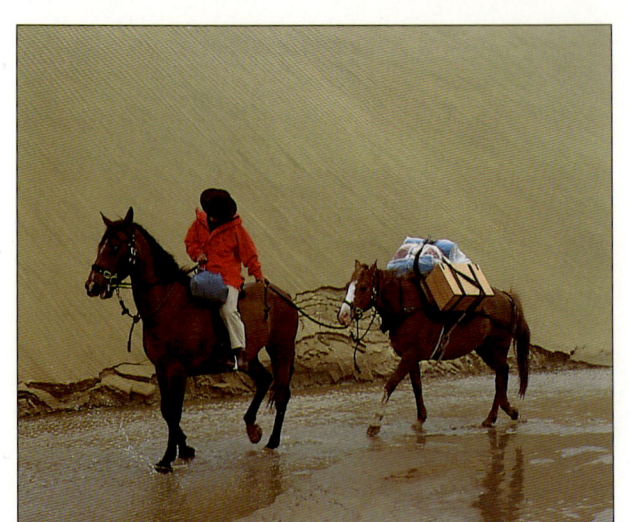

At midnight, our weary troop escaped the maze of dark trees and headed towards a light coming from a small house. A large doberman yanked on his chain, barking ferociously at our approach. Carefully skirting around the full extent of his chain, we knocked apprehensively on the guarded door. We were surprised when a Maori teenage girl in pink flowery pyjamas opened the door. Completely unperturbed by midnight riders she gave permission for our horses to use her grassy paddock and invited Ali and me in to sleep in a very welcome bed!

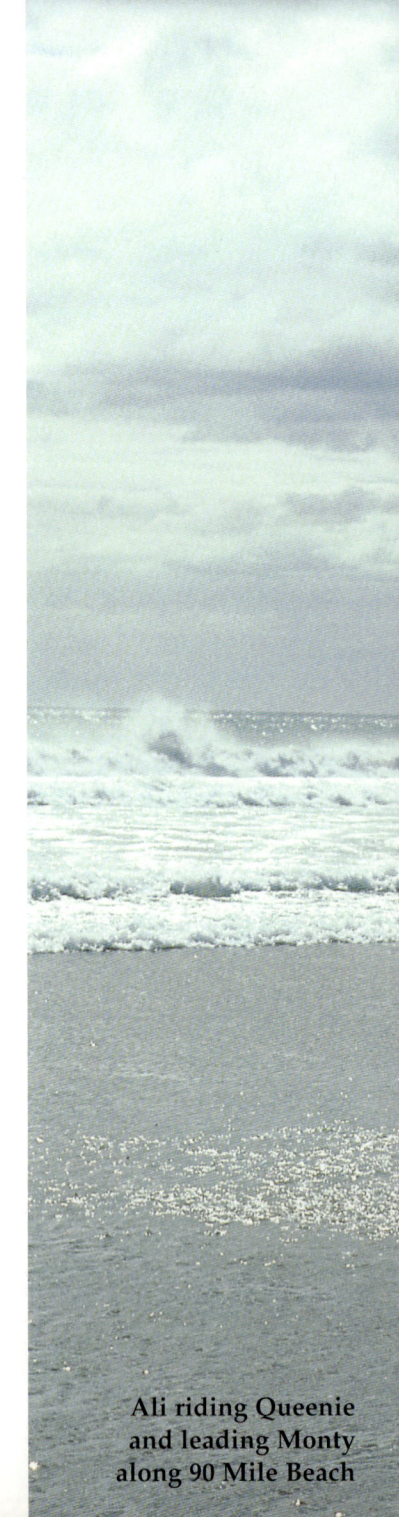

Ali riding Queenie and leading Monty along 90 Mile Beach

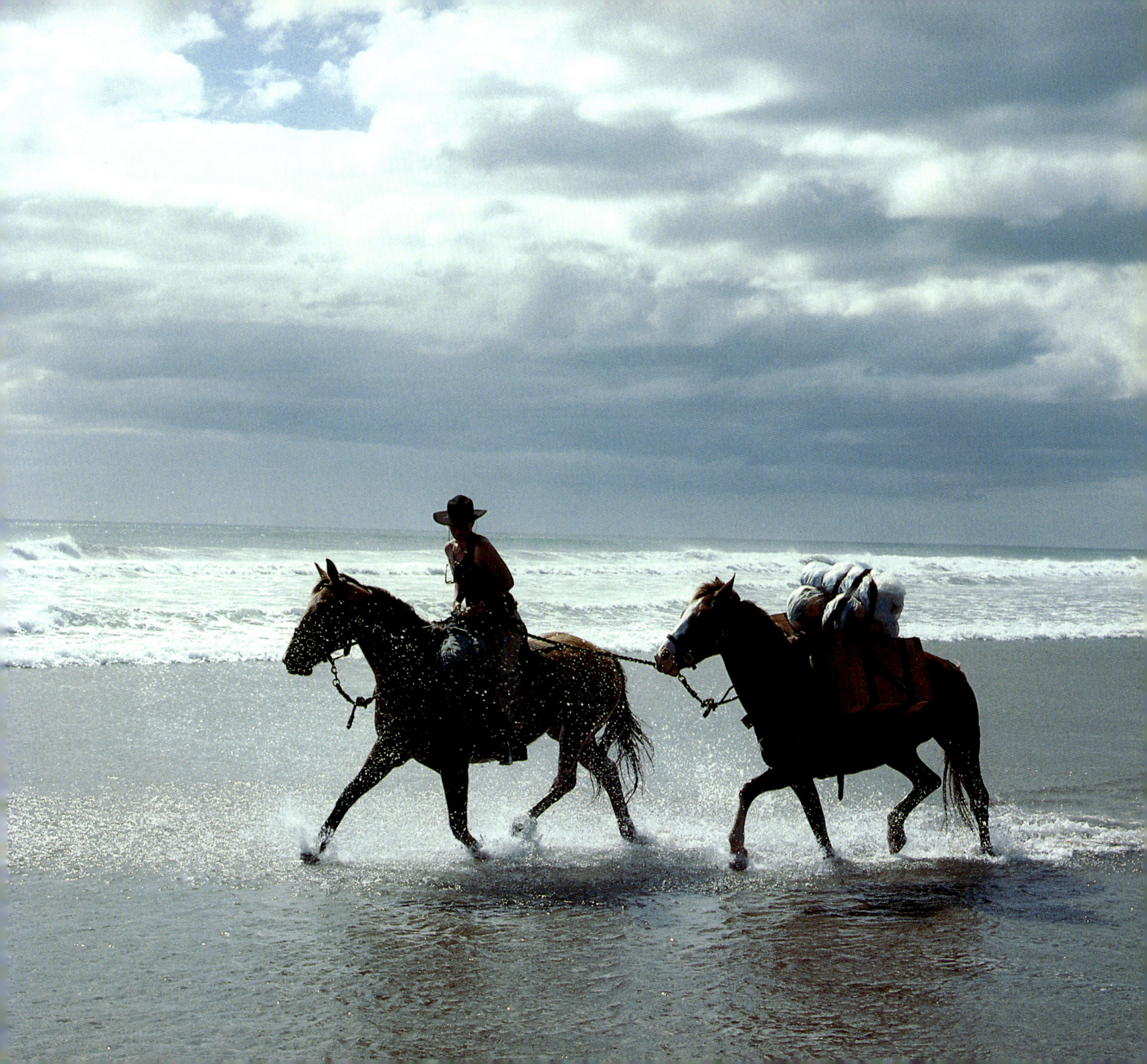

4
AHIPARA

Be strong and take heart, all you who hope in the Lord. Psalm 31:24 NIV

The following day we took a fifteen minute short cut back onto 90 Mile beach and continued southward. Nearing Ahipara, where most of the community lived off their vegetable plots and the sea, we met some friendly Maori fishermen hauling in their nets. They directed us to an orchard, where our horses enjoyed squelching the succulent bright orange tangelo fruit between their teeth while frothy juice dripped from their mouths.

Disaster struck in this idyllic setting. Queenie's lead rope got caught around her hind leg and she came crashing down. We spent several days wrapping her hock with poultices but there was no sign of improvement. We felt gutted, but because of the time restriction on our New Zealand visas, we had no choice but to leave her in the care of friends who agreed to truck her on to us once she had recovered.

Deeply disappointed, leaving our pack with Queenie, we rode on through the rain.

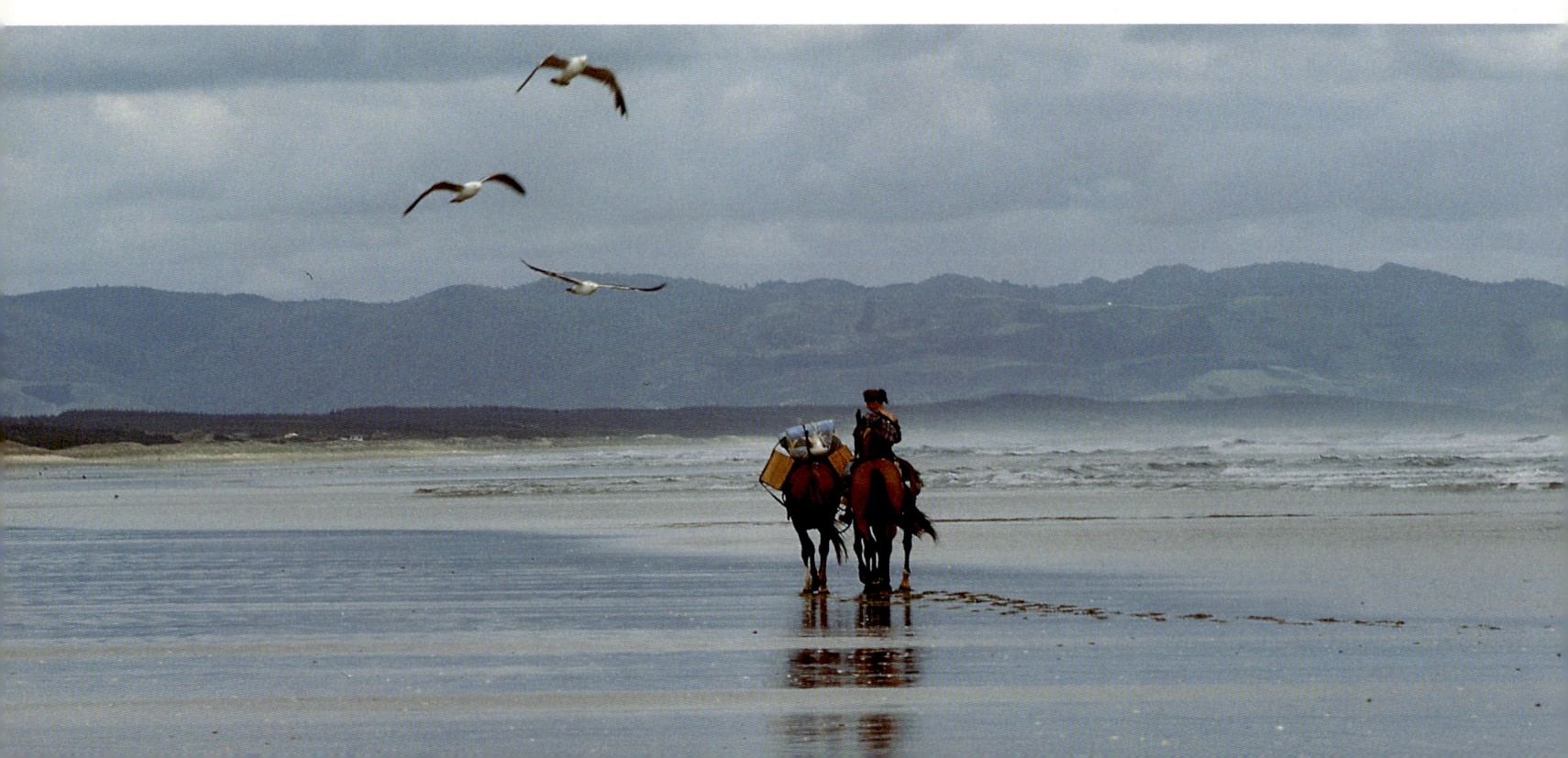

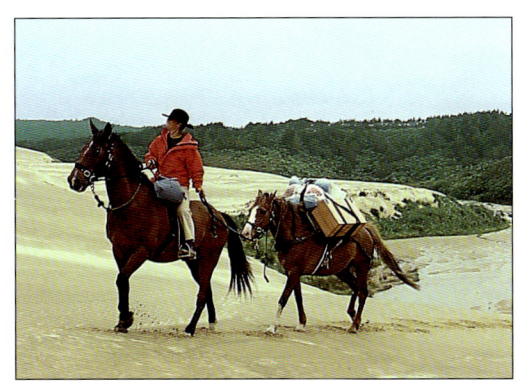 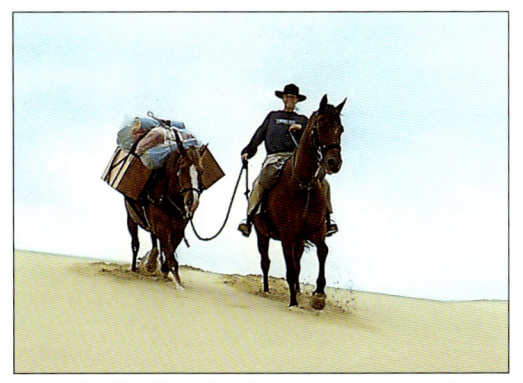 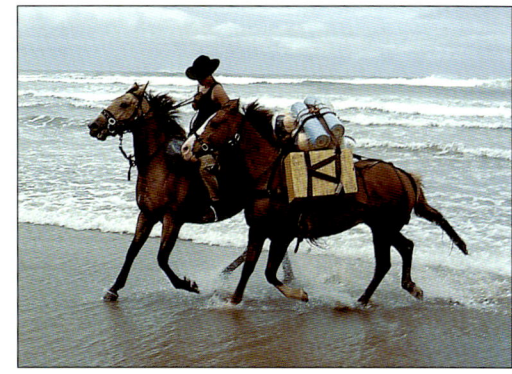

90 Mile Beach - from north to south

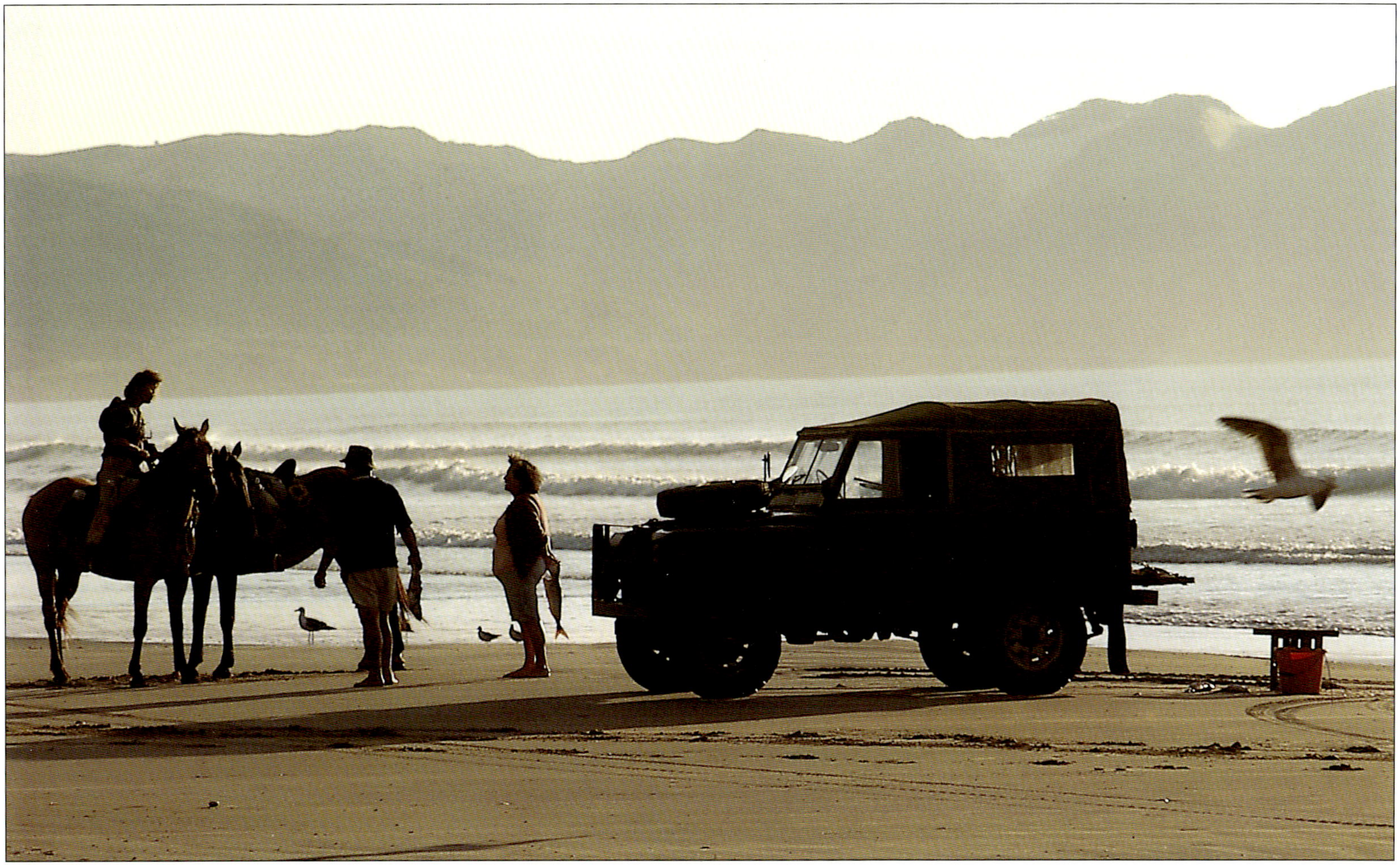

Meeting Maori fishermen near Ahipara

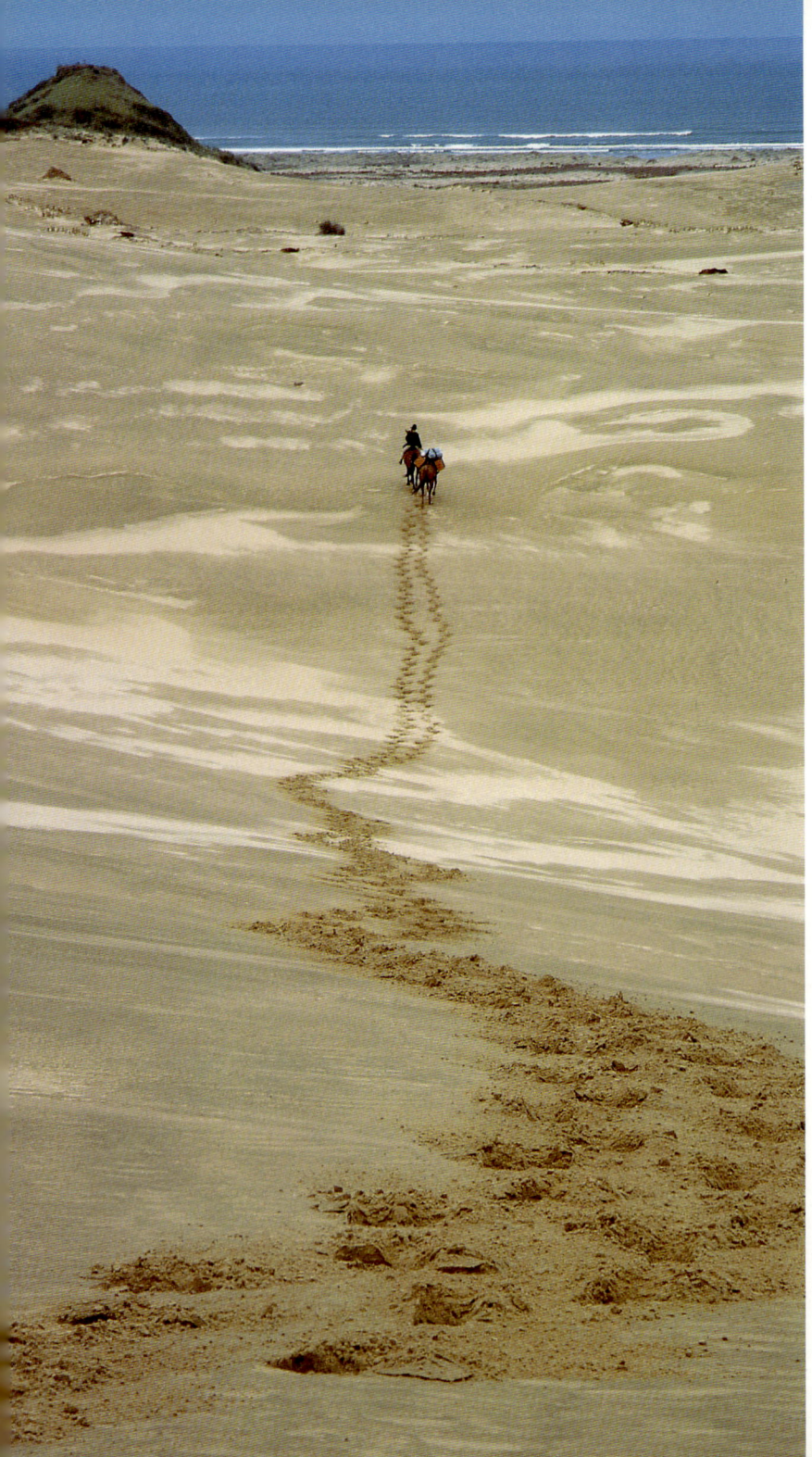

5
Maunganui Bluff

Trust in Him at all times, you people;
Pour out your heart before Him;
God is a refuge for us.
Psalm 62:8 NKJ

The almost tropical North is renowned for its citrus fruit, giant Kauri trees and an abundance of rain. When it rains, it really rains. We soon discovered this when we pitched our small tent on a village rugby pitch, the following morning it appeared to be floating on a lake!

It was dark when we arrived at Maunganui Bluff bordering the sea. The sound of barking dogs directed us to the station where, for a week, we helped out mustering cattle, waiting for Queenie to rejoin us. But she never did. Our friends told us they'd had her x-rayed and found her injury was serious and that she would never be sound enough to participate in our strenuous trek. We felt devastated and couldn't believe our pretty little mare hadn't recovered and that we would have to leave her behind. We needed three horses, but due to our diminishing budget we had to find an inexpensive replacement.

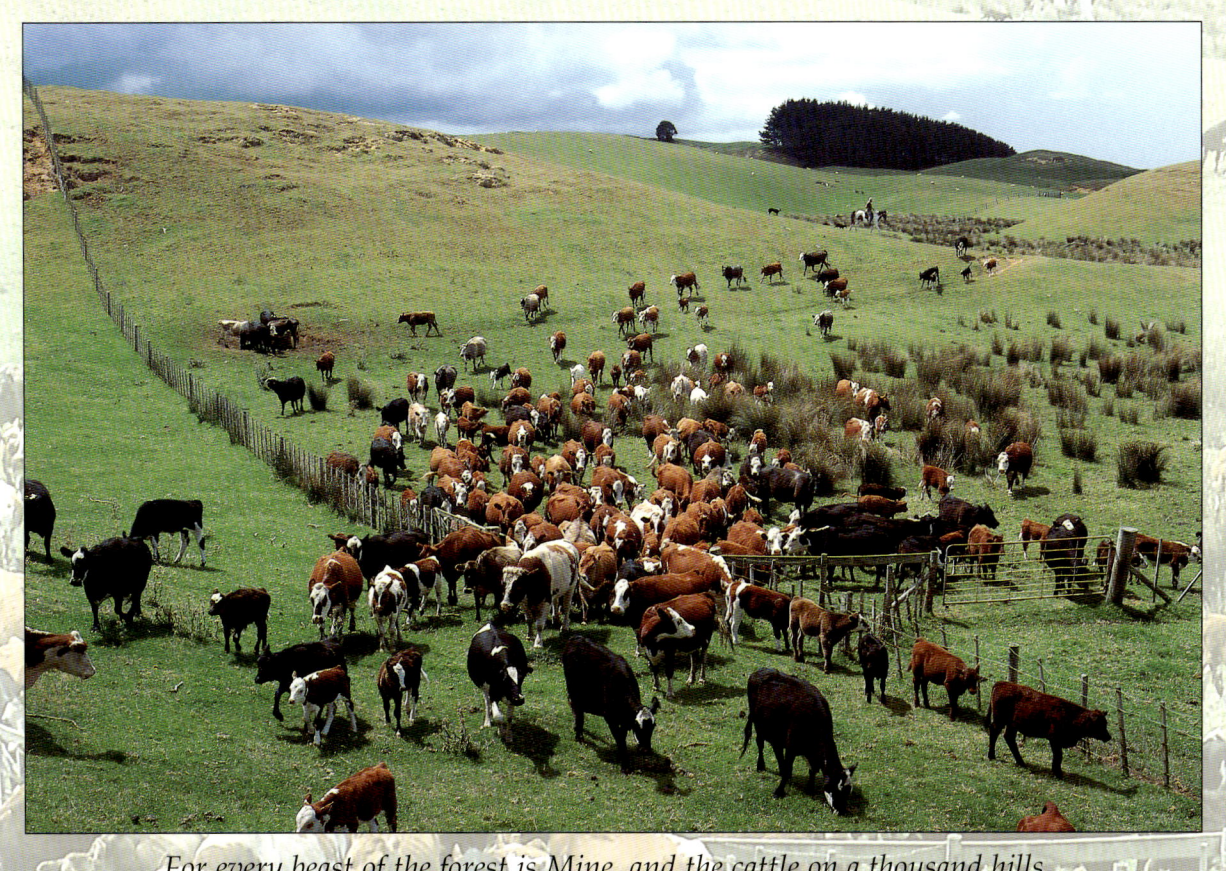

For every beast of the forest is Mine, and the cattle on a thousand hills.
Psalm 50:10 NKJ

Don Harrison moving cattle on his station near Maunganui Bluff

6
AUCKLAND

It is God who arms me with strength, and makes my way perfect. Psalm 18:32 NKJ

Roman was our replacement. A young chestnut gelding, who had been hand raised as an orphan. He was extremely slow but bomb-proof! Ideal for our fund-raising escapade across the sprawling city of Auckland the day before Christmas Eve!

I felt we should be dressed in armour, going into battle as we rode our military trio, Nelson, Monty and Roman into the frenzy of Auckland. A city in a region where two-thirds of New Zealand's population live, wedged between the Tasman Sea and the Pacific Ocean on a narrow neck of land sprawling southward. It was like an electric shock to our senses, after the quiet solitude of Northland.

Trucks and impatient motorists skimmed past us, often blasting their horns, frightening our horses. Relieved, we found a quieter place to fund raise outside Woolworths, until we were ordered off the premises by a beefy security guard. Back on the street, one of us struggled with three horses amidst the heavy traffic, while the other collected for Tearfund, and we were met with many comments like,

"I reckon Bangladesh need all the horse meat they can get!"

"Why don't you cut your horses up and send them to Bangladesh?"

"Do you want to buy some partially legalised marijuana?"

"I'll give you some money, if you give me a kiss!"

Although we also met some more amicable people, the stress of trying to cross a city safely with three horses had given us throbbing headaches and we longed to escape the frenetic concrete jungle. The problem was that the only way out of Auckland southward was motorway, far too dangerous to even consider riding along. We sought refuge on One Tree Hill, an extinct volcano, and an island of tranquillity amidst the humming city and puzzled about what we could possibly do with our horses overnight.

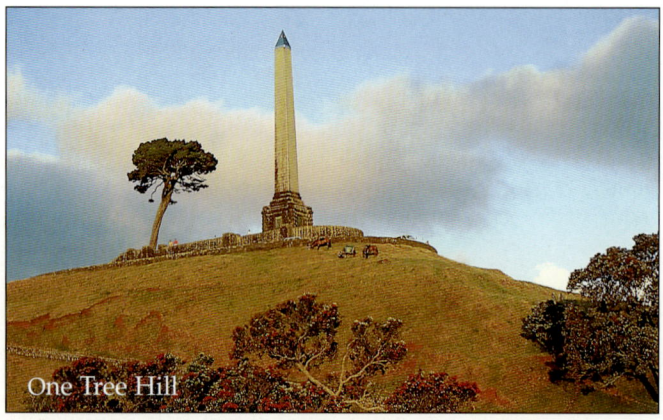
One Tree Hill

Auckland: and Nelson's turn to wear the fund-raising rug while Tracey rode Monty, the pack horse and Ali rode bomb-proof Roman.

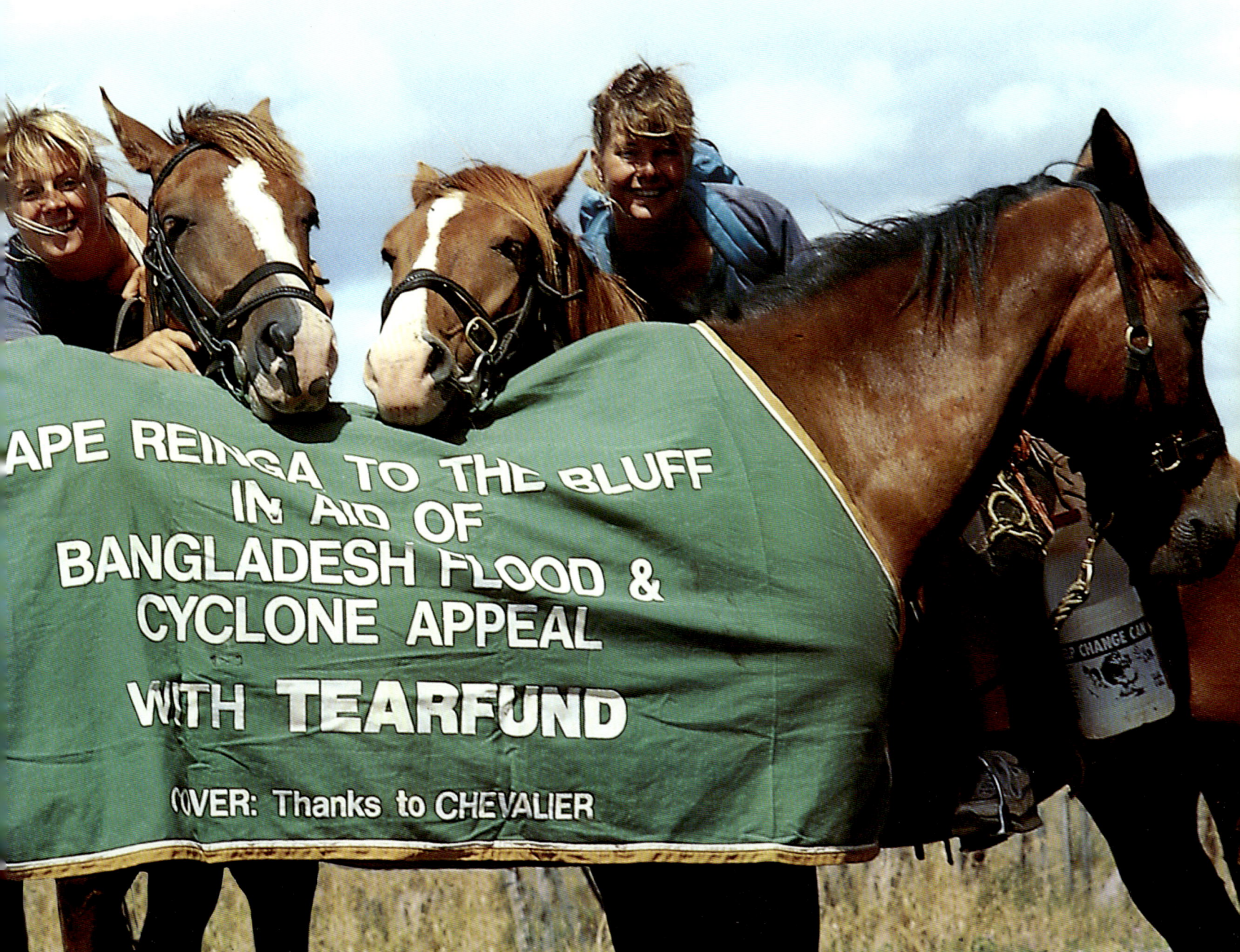

7
3 Lunches!

But he knows the way that I take. Job 23:10 NIV

As our horses' hooves echoed along a residential street in the extensive city a loud diesel truck rattled up behind us. It stopped abreast of us and the driver greeted us with,
   "I heard you girls needed a lift!"
   It was wonderful to be out of Auckland and riding in the quiet country again! Although our progress was slow with many stops along the gravel coastal roads as we frequently had to dismount to remove stones from our horses' hooves. Once, I was removing a stone from Roman's hoof, when suddenly, seeing a mare and foal cavorting on the hillside, he took off through a gate and galloped up a track with saddle bags bouncing and oranges shooting out of the open flaps!   Ali and I both stood amazed that Roman possessed such energy and then burst into laughter.
   "That would have been a good picture!" I exclaimed, "if he hadn't galloped off with my cameras!"
He shortly reappeared over the hill, anxiously nickering to Nelson and Monty, whom he suddenly realised he'd left behind. Following him was a Maori with several of our oranges in his hands, concerned that we were all right.
   The New Zealand people were so hospitable. Although we were always on the move we put on weight in the North Island. One day we had three lunches! A couple we had stayed with overnight sent us off with sandwiches which we gratefully tucked into our saddlebags. Reaching a church, we tied our horses outside, and, dressed like cowgirls went in for the Sunday morning service. Afterwards we were invited to lunch, which was several miles further along our route. As we began to eat our packed lunch some dairy farmers, with whom we had stayed earlier, appeared with more sandwiches. After sharing them with our horses we rode on, to eat our third Sunday lunch with the pastor and his wife.

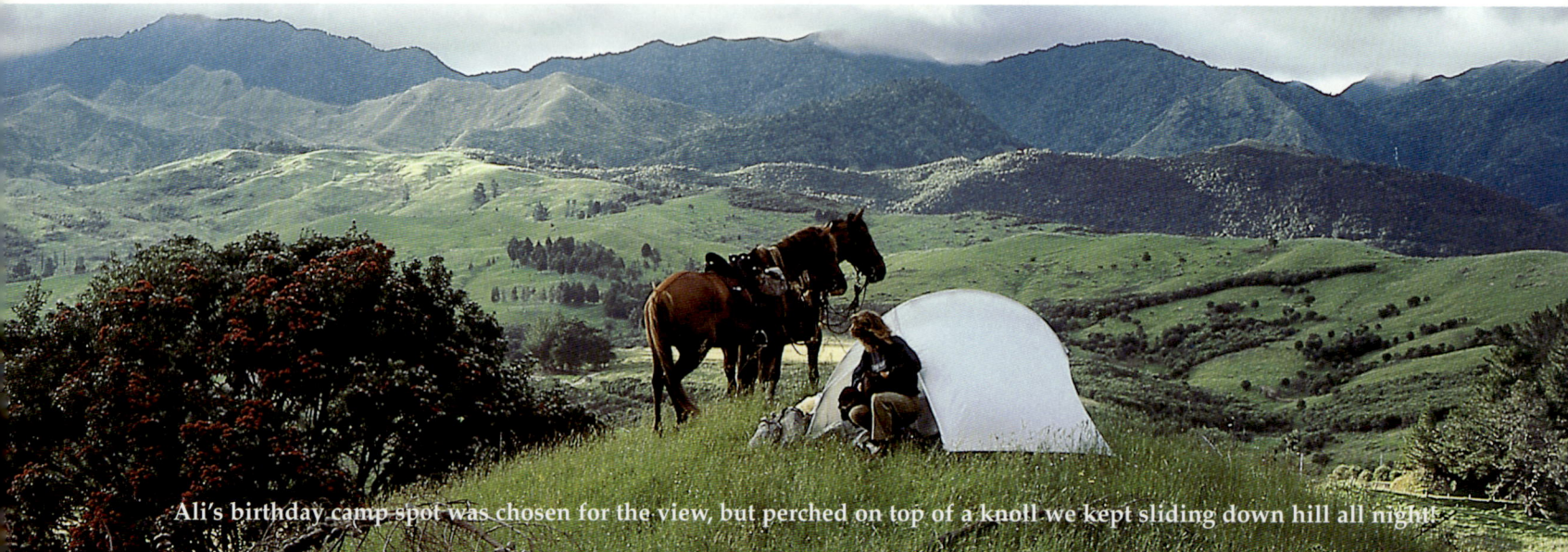
Ali's birthday camp spot was chosen for the view, but perched on top of a knoll we kept sliding down hill all night!

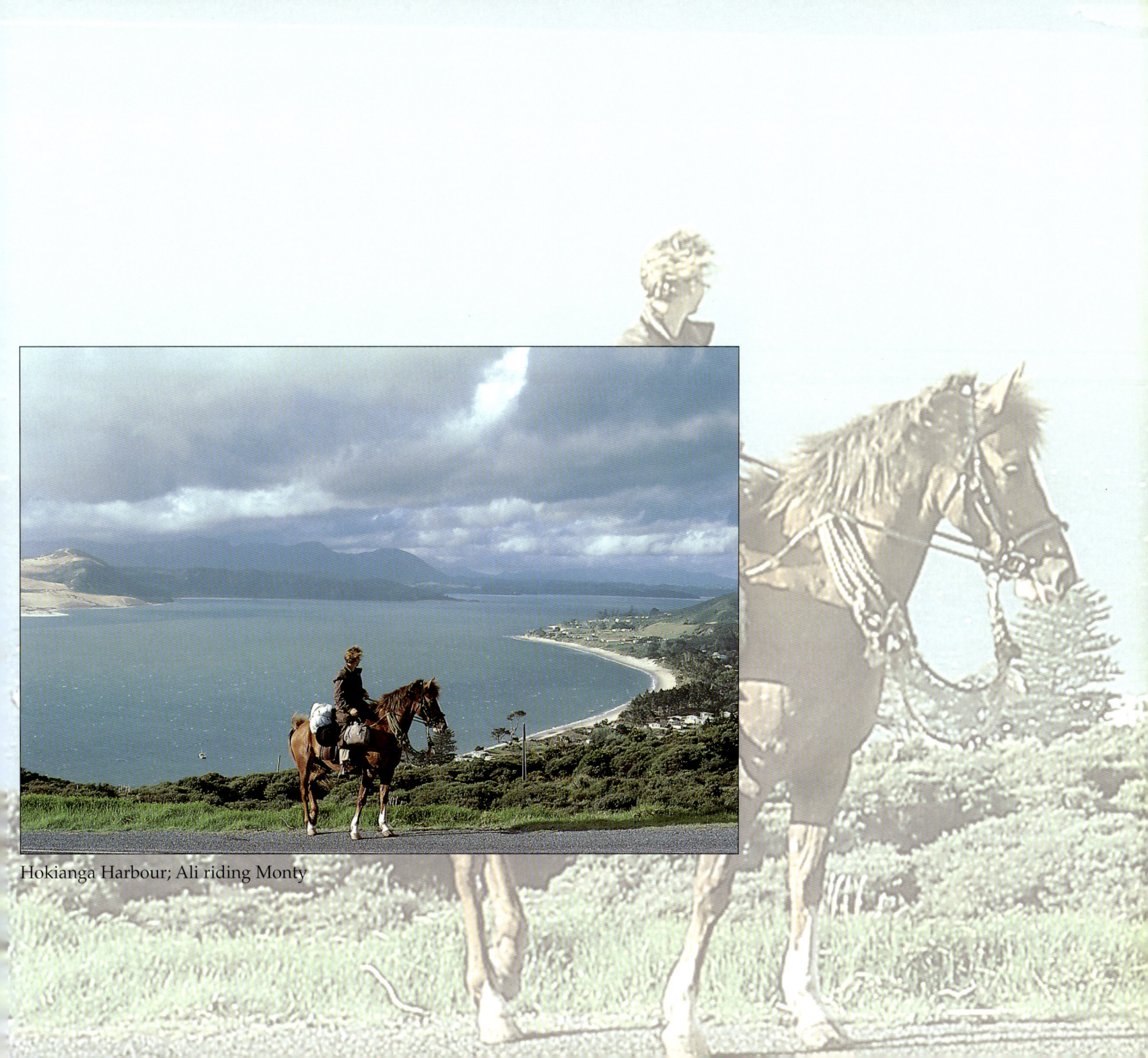

Hokianga Harbour; Ali riding Monty

8
CHRISTMAS DAY

You will show me the path of life; In Your presence is fullness of joy; At Your right hand are pleasures forevermore.
Psalm 16:11 NKJ

On Christmas Day I woke up in our tiny tent pitched by the sea, to find one of Ali's ankle socks bulging with sweets on my sleeping bag. I was grateful for the Christmas stocking and also that the sock was clean as our wardrobe was very limited! It was a beautiful summer's day as we followed the Coromandel Coastline south, spying out a good spot to spend Christmas Day. We turned off the winding gravel road and splashed down a stream to a secluded beach. It was an ideal spot with fresh water and grass shaded by a majestic red flowering pohutukawa tree for our horses and a sunny stretch of sand for us. After washing our horses down and Ali enjoying a swim with Roman, our horses grazed contentedly in the shade while we sat on the warm sand, looking across the sparkling azure water to the smoky blue Coromandel Peninsula. In this idyllic place we ate our Christmas lunch, a plateful of mince pies we had been given earlier that morning.

Later that day we took a quick plunge in the icy river for a wash before accepting an invitation to a family barbecue further along the beach. We left Monty lying down resting while Nelson and Roman grazed contentedly. We returned an hour later. All three had vanished!

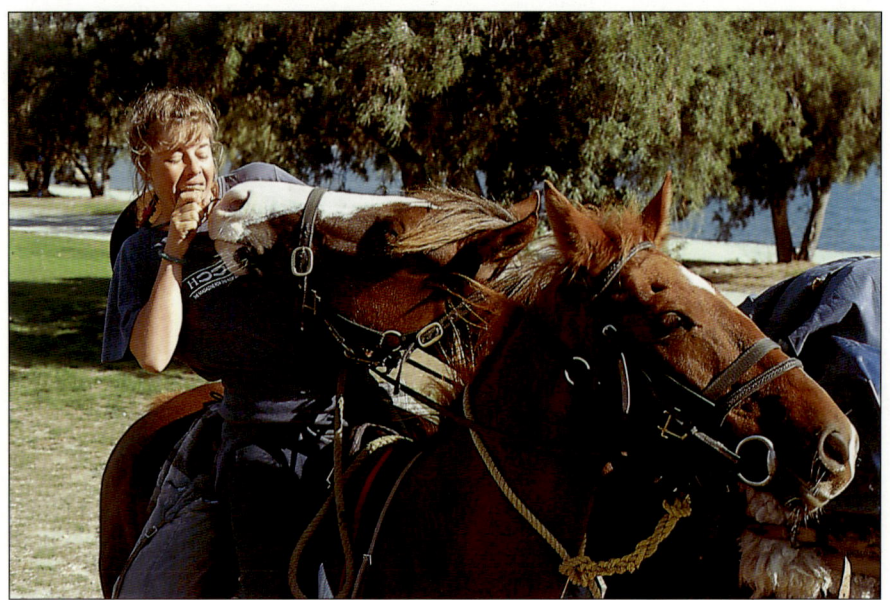

Monty wants Ali's ice cream!

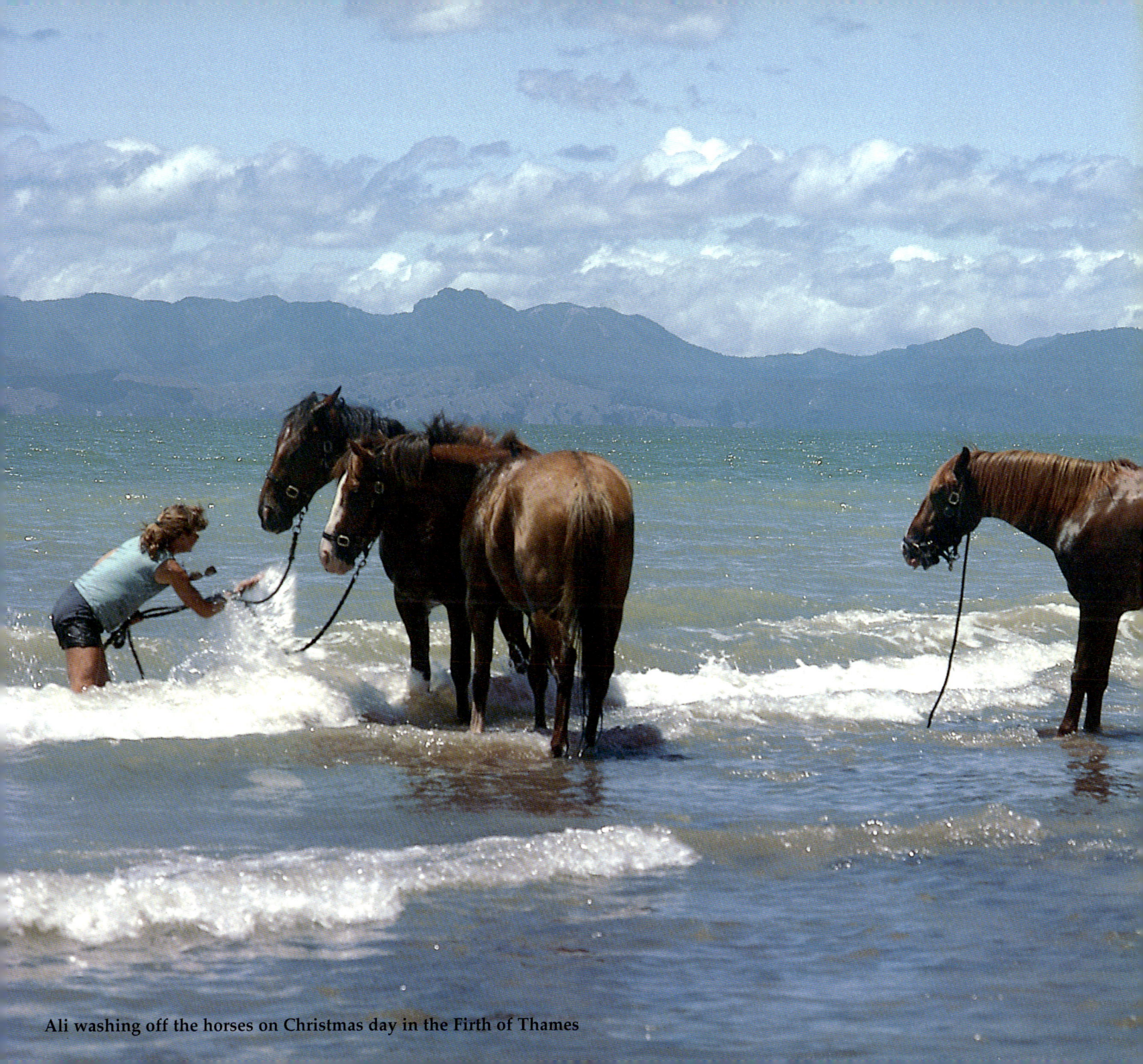
Ali washing off the horses on Christmas day in the Firth of Thames

9
3 Horses!

We don't know what to do, but we are looking to you. 2 Chronicles 20:12 TLB

Barefoot, dressed in our long T-shirts, which doubled as beach and night wear, we retraced our route back up the river that we had ridden down earlier that day, expecting to find the horses just round each bend. But they weren't there. Our prayers became more urgent as we hurried over the sharp stones, too concerned about our horses getting hit by a vehicle on the twisting gravel roads to waste time going back to dress. Our track came to a T-junction so we split up, going in opposite directions. A car came speeding round the corner and I frantically waved it down.

"Have you seen three horses?" I asked desperately. The driver shook her head. "Please could you give me a lift to find them?' I pleaded and I felt her eyes drop from my Snoopy T-shirt to my bare feet. "Just to the first house!"

"O.K," she relented, "just to the first house." Before she had time to change her mind I had squeezed into her mini amongst her menagerie of dogs, cats, and a large bird cage. I caught snippets as she chatted about heading home for Christmas as I intently scanned the twisting road and verges for our horses... after a few miles she dropped me at the first house.

Barefoot on the doorstep, my knock was answered by a tall young man holding a glass of wine, obviously surprised and puzzled by my appearance out of nowhere!

"Have you seen three horses? We've lost our horses!"

"No, I'm sorry !" he replied, turning to call over his shoulder to a group of people sitting in a room festooned in Christmas decorations.

"Anyone here seen some loose horses?" he asked, and I saw various members of the family look enquiringly in my direction shaking their heads. He apologetically confirmed that no one had seen any and I thanked him as he closed the door.

It was getting dark and I had no idea where Ali was and it was going to be a long painful walk, barefoot along the gravel roads back to the junction where we had separated. I suddenly felt a wave of homesickness come over me, as I stood on the doorstep. In the dusk I whispered, " Now what, God"?

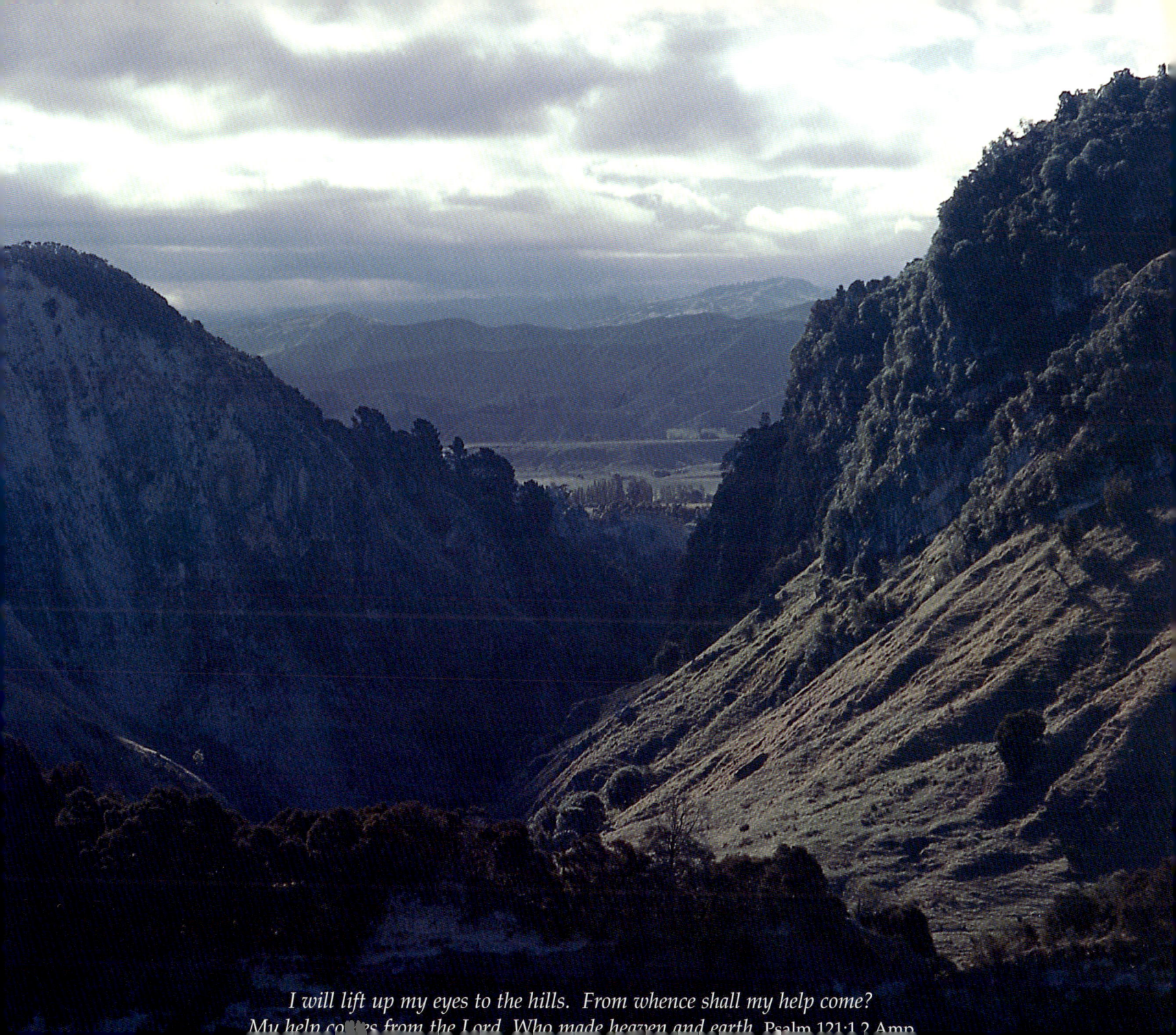

I will lift up my eyes to the hills. From whence shall my help come? My help comes from the Lord, Who made heaven and earth. Psalm 121:1,2 Amp.

10
LOST AND FOUND!

Whoever trusts in the Lord, happy is he. Proverbs 16:20 NKJ

I gazed absently across the darkening valley beneath me, at livestock and some horses grazing. In an instant my eyes snapped back to the horses, focusing intently through the gloom. Those dark silhouettes seemed familiar, but how would they have got down there?

A certainty rose up inside me and barefooted I clambered over the wire fence and oblivious to the rough ground I raced down the hill towards them. A car with glaring headlights arrived simultaneously and out hopped Ali! She had met the man who found them on the road and put them in the paddock for safety - The timing of God!

Elated, we jumped on our horses and riding bareback in the moonlight we took an alternative route back to our campsite along a beach, singing our praises to God. Our joyful Christmas carols were only punctuated by moments of concentration as our horses shied away from the driftwood scattered across the illuminated sand.

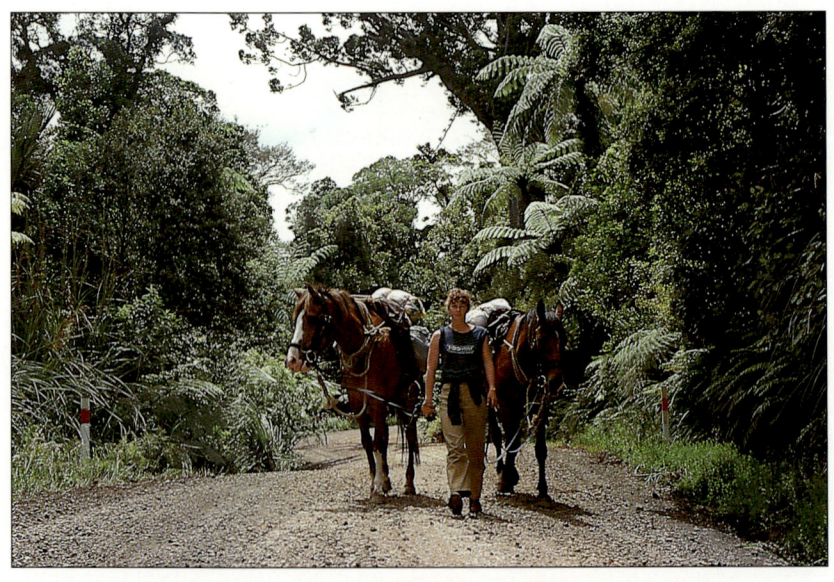

We walked several hours a day to give the horses a break.

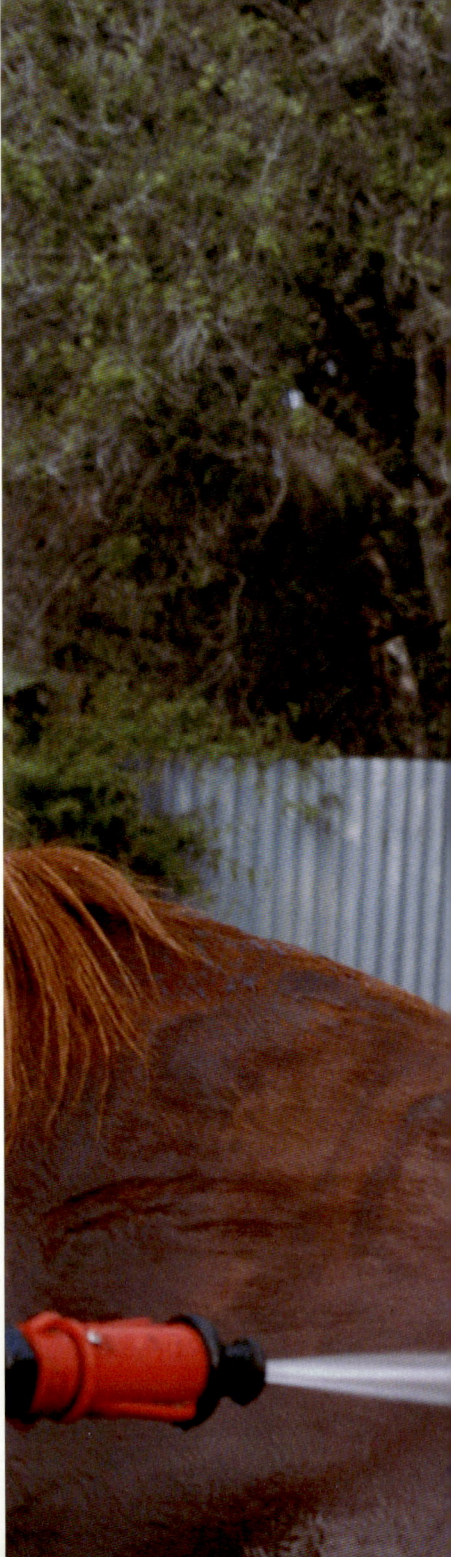

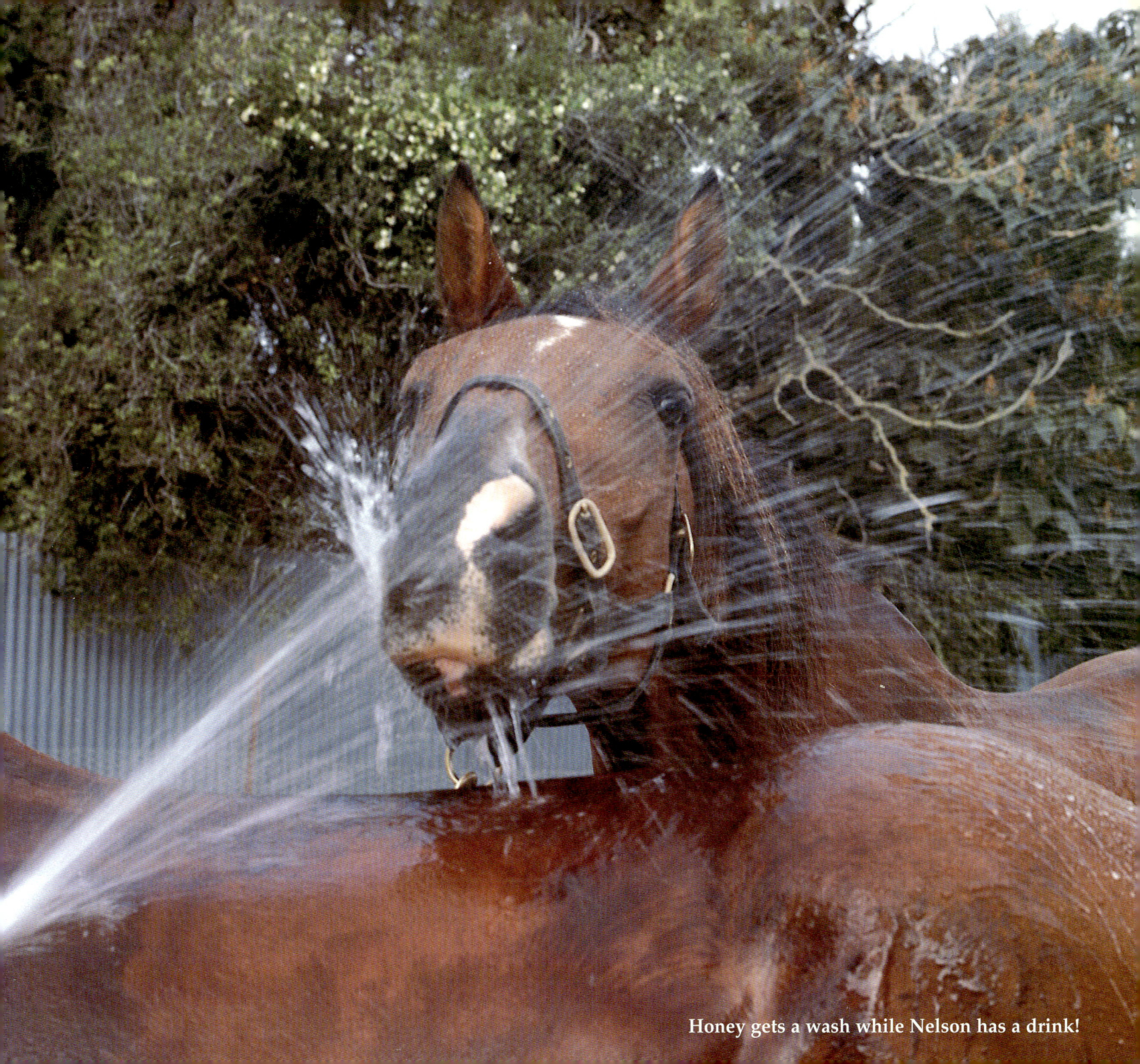

Honey gets a wash while Nelson has a drink!

11
NO HOOF NO HORSE

So we're not giving up. How could we!
Even though on the outside it often looks like things are falling apart on us. 2 Corinthians 4:16 TM

The day after Christmas, as we led our horses south along the Coromandel Peninsula, we were only 300 miles into our trek but it looked like the end.

Every week we had to get the horses re-shod as their shoes continually wore out. The numerous nail holes had seriously perforated the hoof wall, causing them to disintegrate to the point where it was impossible to re-shoe them. Roman added to this problem by dragging the tips of his hind hooves and this had almost worn away the protective hoof wall. It is a true equestrian saying, " No hoof no horse".

To prolong the wear of the shoes we wearily led our horses along the softer grass verges, wilting into the mirage of heat wavering before us. A truck coming from another direction met us at a junction and a large man climbed out and strolled over to us.

"I've heard about you gals," he remarked and then immediately caught sight of our shoeing problem. "He'll be through to blood soon!" He ran his large hand down Roman's leg.

"If you come back to my place, I'll fix you up if you like!" he invited. We were sceptical as several other farriers had previously promised they could fix our shoeing problem. It had cost us a lot of money we could ill afford and the shoes continued to wear out just as quickly. He also lived in a different direction from where we were heading and the horses' shoes just wouldn't take them that extra 20 miles.

"Thank you, but we are heading in the other direction." Ali explained.

The truck roared off and left us in a haze of fumes and I wondered if we had made the right decision as we continued plodding on into the evening. Eventually we arrived at a T-junction but we couldn't decide which was the best road to take, so we stopped, unsaddled the horses and flopped down on the grass while the horses grazed around us. Too exhausted even to think what to do next.

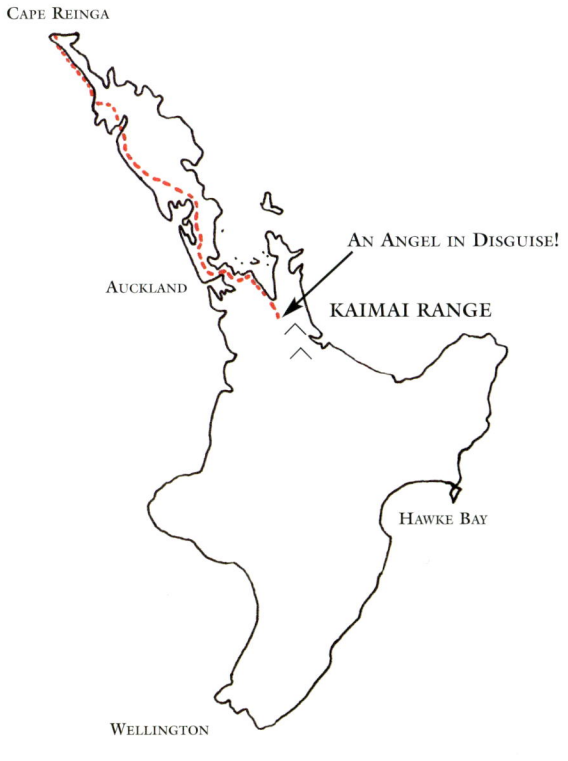

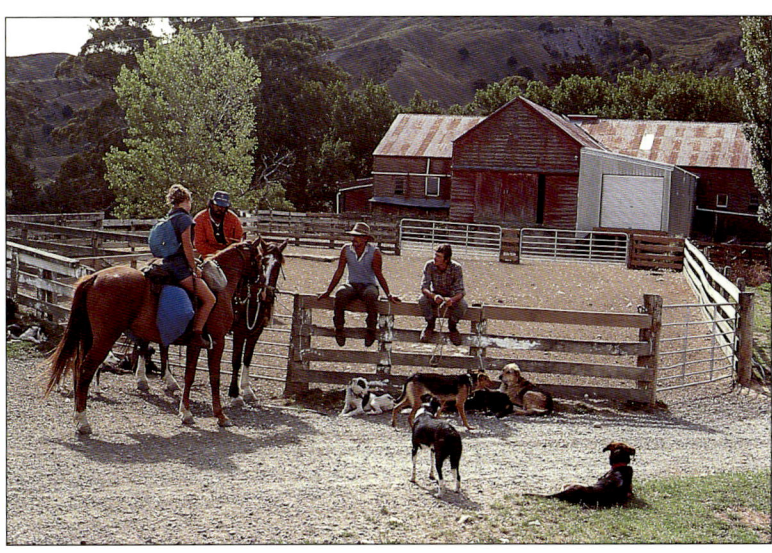

Meeting some sheep musterers.

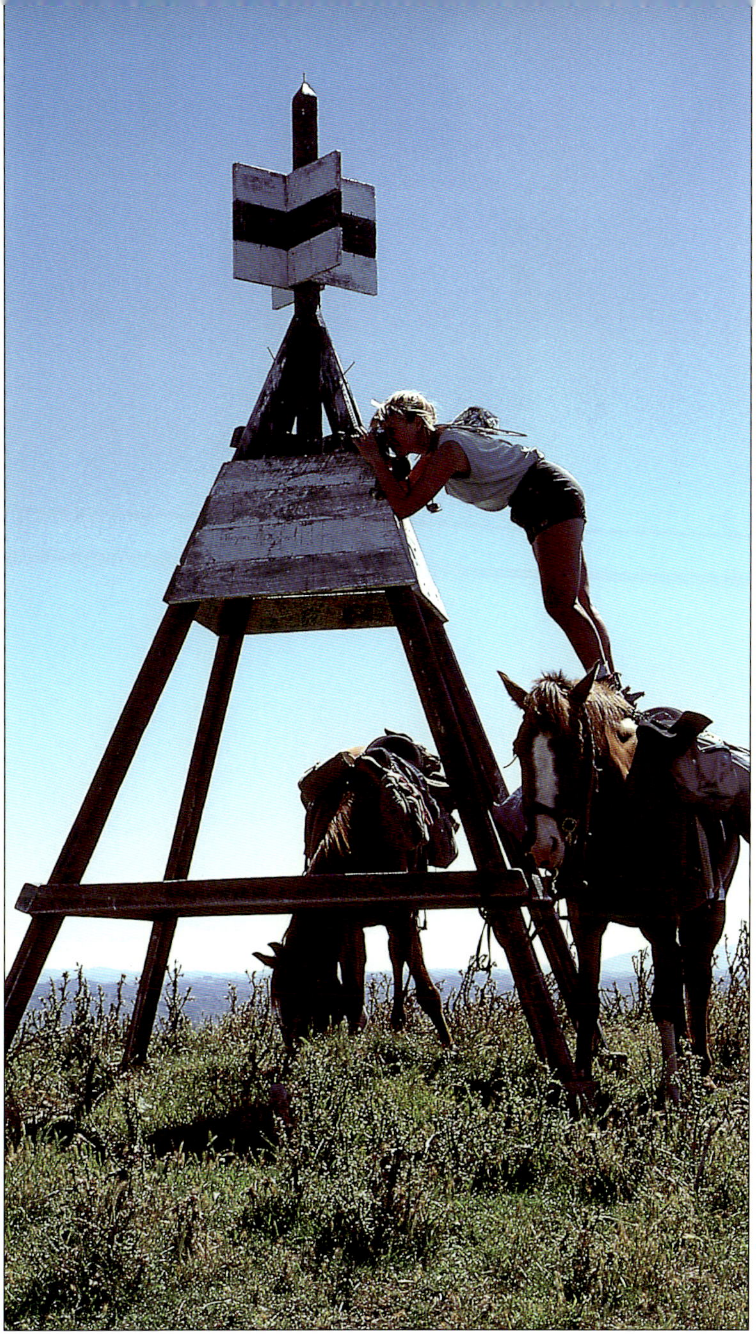

Tracey standing on Monty while using a trig. point as a tripod for a self timed photo. But 10 seconds was the maximum her old Olympus OM1 camera offered. On this attempt it was not long enough to get into position!

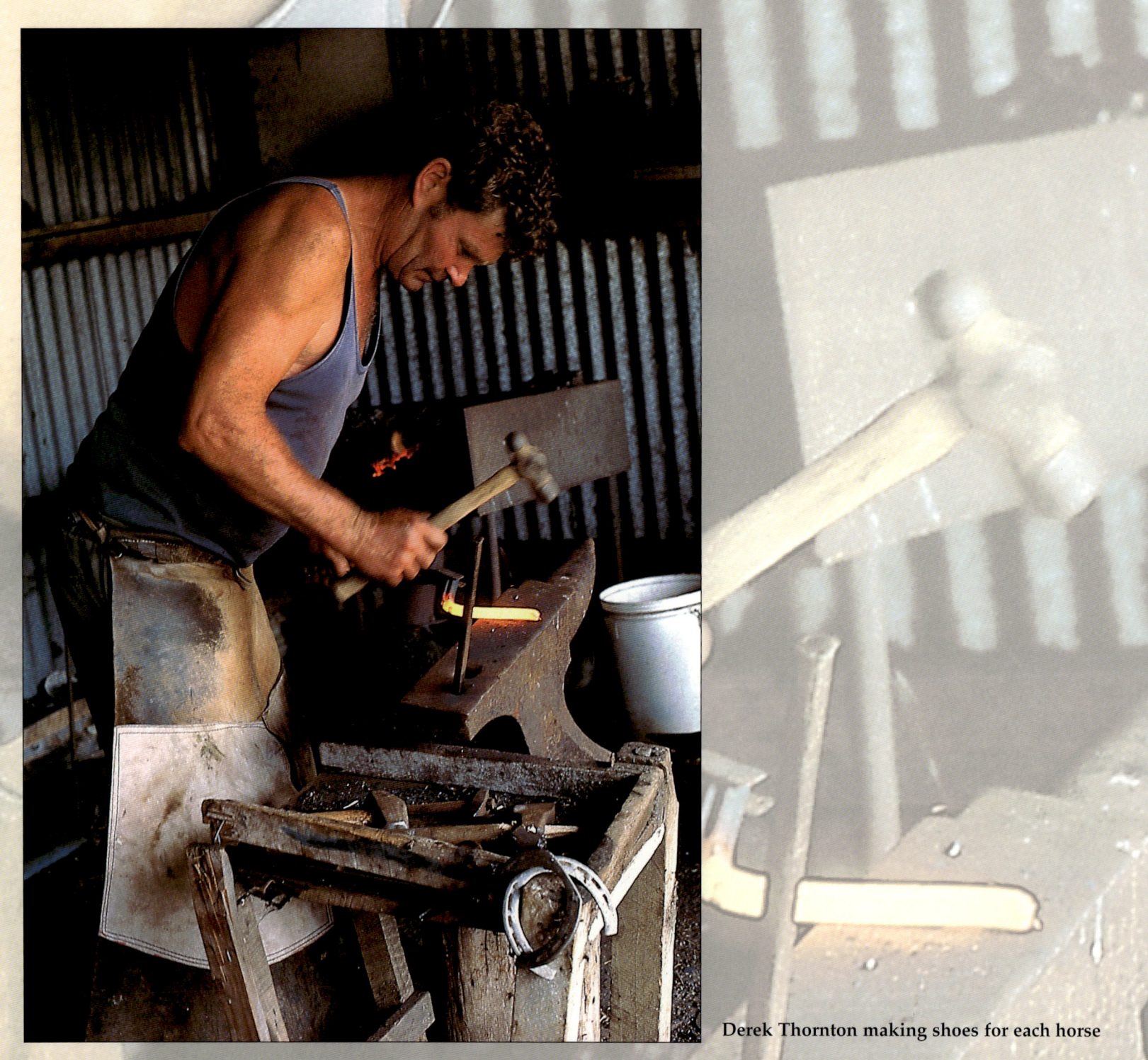

Derek Thornton making shoes for each horse

12
AN ANGEL IN DISGUISE!

A man's steps are of the Lord; How then can a man understand his own way?
Proverbs 20:24 NKJ

Lying exhausted on the grass, while the horses grazed around me, I was only conscious of traffic slowing up at the junction and then speeding away. I heard a diesel truck's engine die, a door slam, and as I opened my eyes I could only see the silhouette of a large figure standing over me, blocking out the sun. Startled, I jumped up feeling dizzy.

"You girls are coming home with me and I'll have no arguments!" I recognised Derek Thornton the man we had met earlier in the afternoon. He had driven 40 miles to drop off his horses and come back to get us!
We didn't decline this time! Instead, quickly gathering our scattered equipment we loaded our horses into his truck. Having travelled so slowly it was quite an uncanny sensation being in a vehicle travelling so much faster! Derek drove us home and his wife Jimmi fed us huge working men's meals while Derek forged a tailor-made set of shoes for each of our horses. He welded hard rod metal on to the shoe surfaces and made reinforced toe clips for Roman. This was the miracle which enabled us to continue our trek! From then on, we always had hard rod metal welded on to the shoes and they lasted three times longer.

Derek with his mumbled stream of bad language refused any payment. Our angel in disguise!

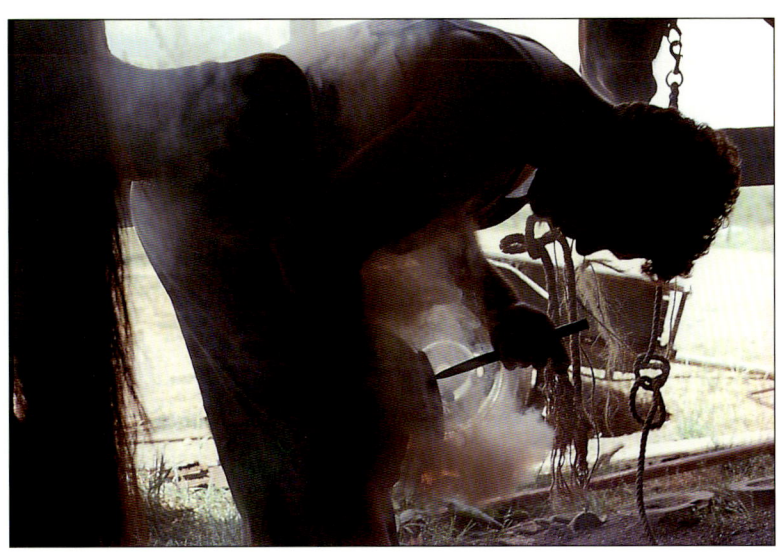
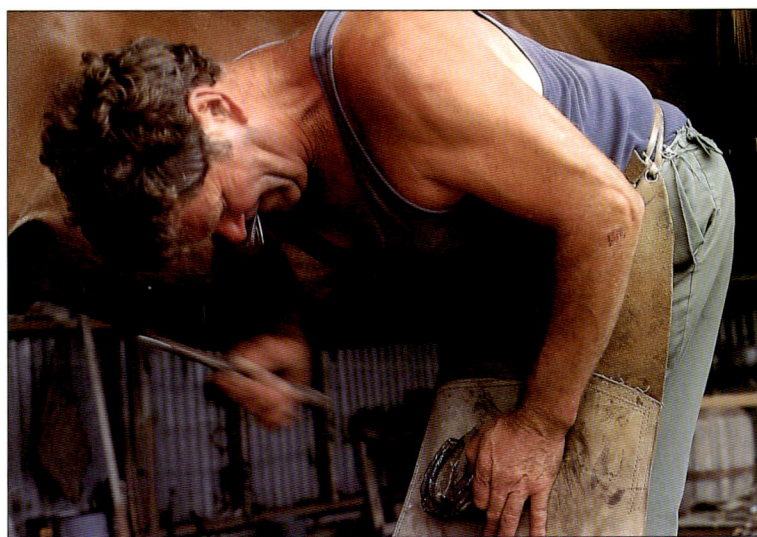

For the Lord God will help me; Therefore I will not be disgraced; Therefore I have set my face like a flint.
Isaiah 50:7 NKJ

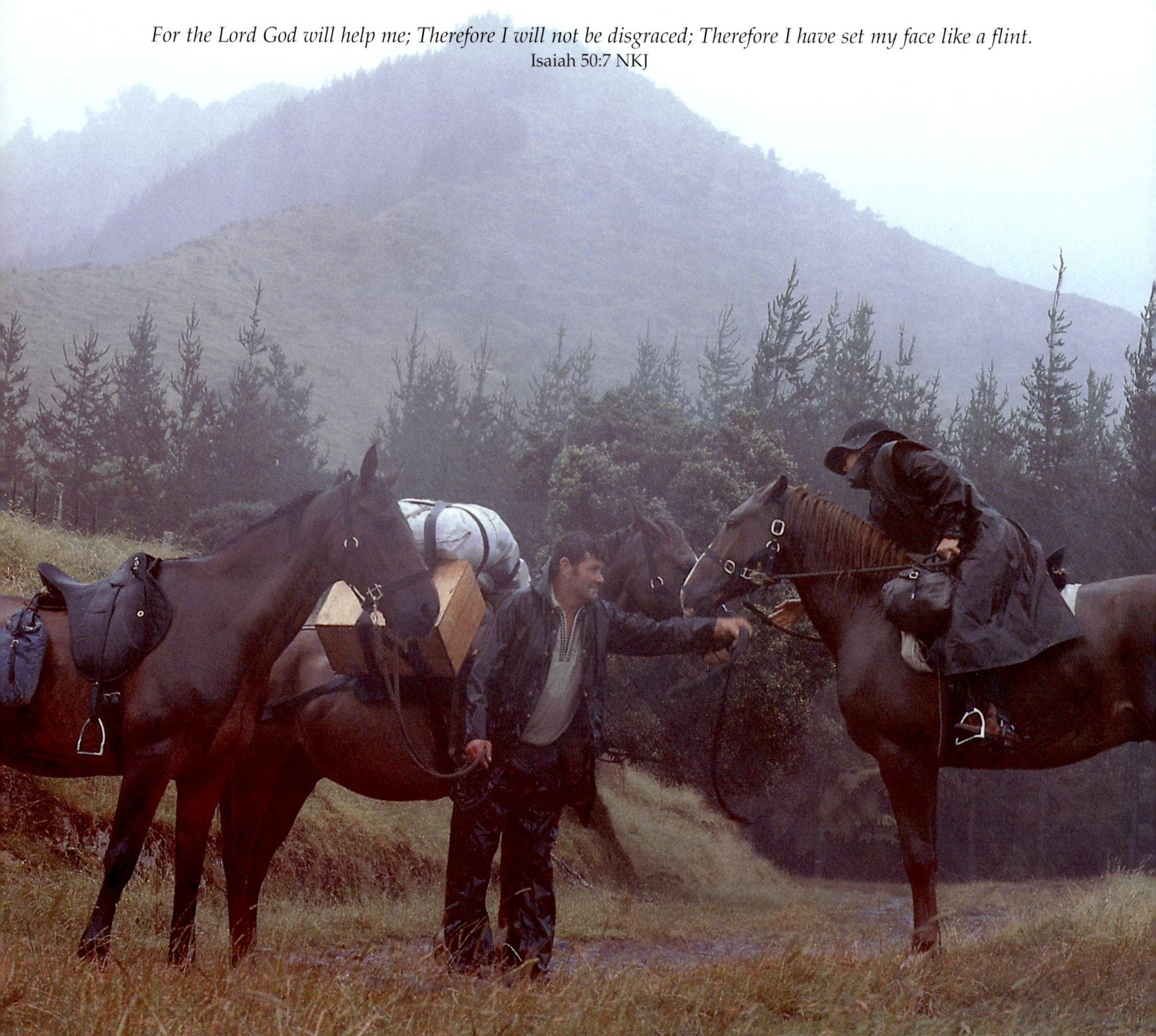

13
CYCLONE

O my soul, march on in strength!
Judges 5:21 NKJ

With three sets of spanking new shoes, Derek dropped us back on our route at the base of the Kaimai hills in raging wind and rain, whereupon we discovered we had left our bridles behind!

"There's a cyclone on its way!" He mumbled and swore, trying to dissuade us, adding, "And anyway, how are you going to manage without bridles?"

'It'll be difficult but we will!" I assured both myself and him and he agreed to send them on to us.

"Thank you so much for everything but we do have to get going!" Ali explained. "We're more than a month behind schedule and we don't know if well make it to Bluff before our visas expire again."

The higher we climbed over the Kaimai Range, the harder the rain hit us as we slid in the mud, in and out of overflowing pot-holes. Monty slid uncontrollably, continuously ramming us with the sharp edges of his wooden pack boxes, bruising our legs. Nearing the crest of the divide, the brunt of the wind drove the rain horizontally into our faces. The horses, refusing to continue in the driving rain, kept swivelling their hind quarters into the prevailing weather. On the crest of a range of hills in a cyclone wasn't the place to have a strike! With one hand clinging to our hats and the other to our slippery lead ropes attached only to head collars, which gave us little control, we struggled to coax our horses on, slip-sliding across the Kaimai Range to the Bay of Plenty.

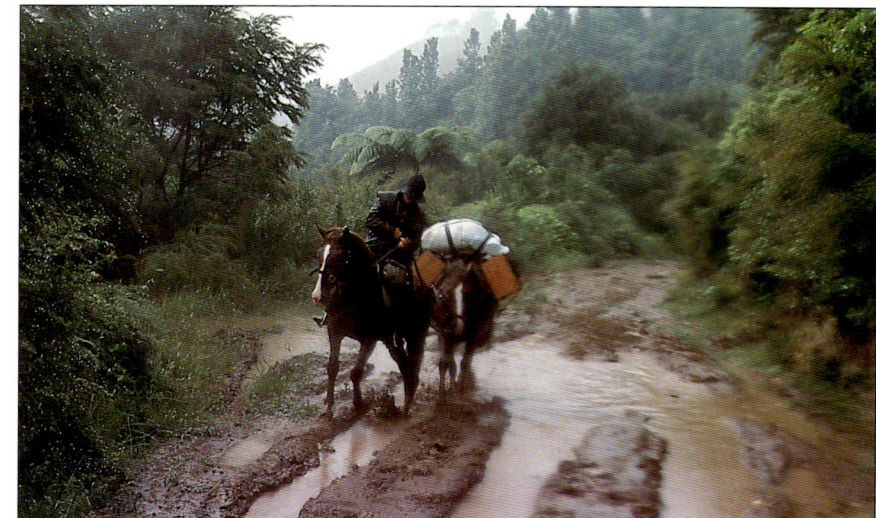

Crossing over the Kaimai Range in the driving rain

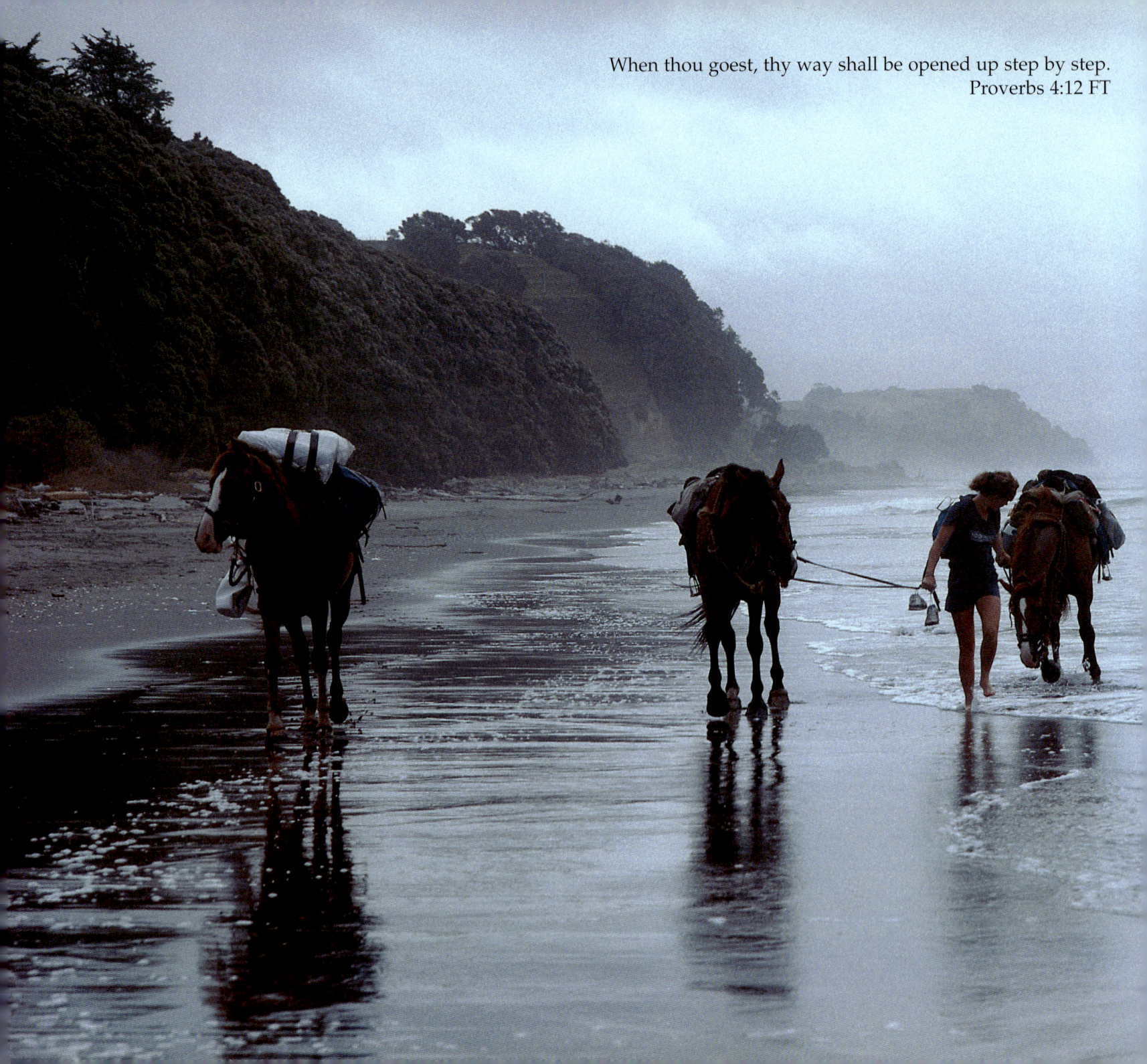
When thou goest, thy way shall be opened up step by step.
Proverbs 4:12 FT

14
REST AND RESPITE

We took shelter from the continuing storm at the Parkers' smallholding near Tauranga. We had stayed with Mary and Angus the previous year, working in the kiwi fruit packing shed while saving for our expedition.

It was wonderful to dry out. We had been damp or wet the majority of our time riding through the humid North and mould had grown on our food and saddlery. In these conditions our horses also collected numerous ticks so we washed them again using a special solution. It was a good opportunity to renew our supplies, which included replacing Monty's wooden pack boxes. Monty was a very companionable horse, but unaware he was so much wider carrying the pack he frequently trotted up behind Nelson and Roman and innocently rammed them in the hindquarters, making them leap forward in shock. He bumped into our sides too and squashed our legs giving us a string of bruises up and down our calves.

We took stock of our finances, realising that we had only done 400 miles of our 2,000 mile expedition and only had a few hundred dollars left. Buying an extra horse and the many shoeing bills had seriously diminished our savings.

"Ali, how long do you think this will last us?" I questioned, having counted out our remaining dollars.

"A few more weeks, if we don't have too many extra expenses." Ali guessed adding, "We'd better pray about it."

As we prepared to leave Tauranga a letter arrived. Before we began our ride Ali and I had taken care of a farm. Its owners had sent us an unexpected payment!

Travelling along the Bay of Plenty coastline.

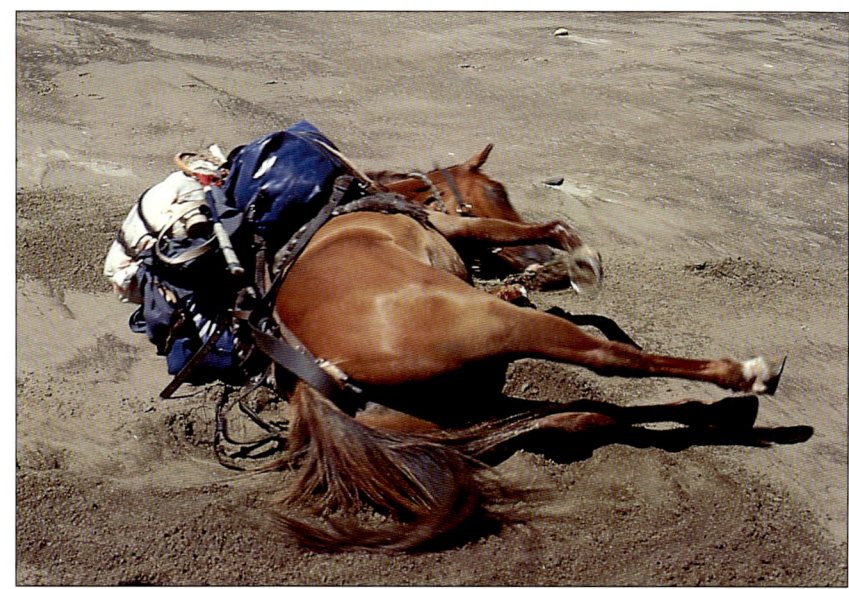

Monty rolls on his new packs, and repeatedly squashes the contents!

15
SHEEPSKINS

Casting all your care upon Him, for He cares for you. (and our horses) 1 Peter 5:7 NKJ

Captain James Cook sailed into this broad sweeping bay in October 1769 and called it the Bay of Plenty because he was able to obtain good supplies from the prosperous Maori villages along the coast.

We waited a week for the rain to abate and then fund raised in Tauranga with the aid of our new super doopa poopa scoop that Angus had designed out of large plastic bottles, for picking up horse droppings in town! Mary had sent us off with neat raisin sandwiches, which we were looking forward to eating, rewarding ourselves at the end of our tiring day's fund raising. But Monty grabbed them first and I had to snatch the last sandwich out of his mouth. Although squashed and covered in green slobber on the outside it was wrapped in cellophane so Ali and I did get to taste one!

Under a heavy grey sky, buffeted by the wind, we rode on, fording the numerous and often deep estuaries strung out across the Bay of Plenty coastline. An eerie looking graveyard lay ahead strewn with bleached driftwood and a few dead penguins that the boisterous sea had spat out on to the sand.

It was in these damp humid conditions that our food and tack grew mouldy and saddle sores developed on our horses. This was a serious hindrance to continuing our trip, so once again we asked God for a solution while we walked for several days in our riding boots which gave us blisters but rested our horses' backs.

"These will do the trick!" Cecil Richardson, a farmer we had stayed with overnight, slung a raw sheepskin, wool side down across Monty's back. The putrid, uncured skins made our stomachs churn, impregnated our saddlery and lingered on our skin and I wondered whether we'd all get fly blown! We put the smelliest on Monty as he preferred to be independent, sometimes hanging back for a mouthful of grass or to roll on our carefully balanced packs squashing the contents. As we travelled the sheepskins dried, the smell faded and soon they became treasured possessions as the natural wool lying against the horses' backs absorbed the sweat and within a few days their backs were healed.

Then one night after we hung them up to dry, they were stolen. The owner of the culprits, thieving station dogs, apologetically gave us several more bloody, smelly, uncured sheepskins with their ears and ear tags still intact! So once again our stomachs churned and we were compelled to breathe through our mouths, as our on-the-move curing process began all over again!

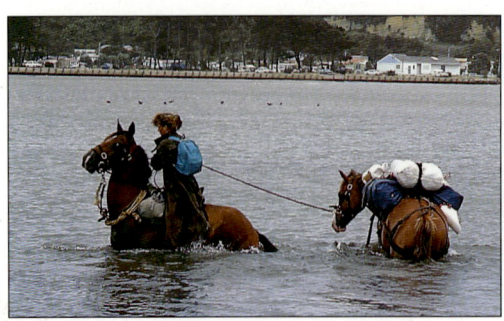
Fording the Little Waihi estuary at low tide.

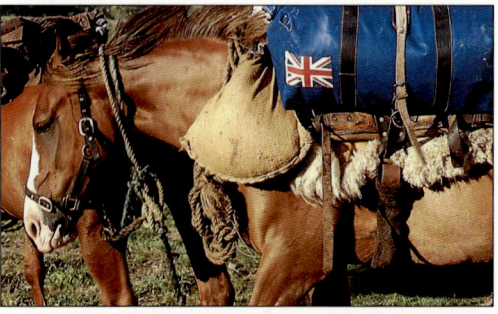
Monty wearing his sheepskin under the pack.

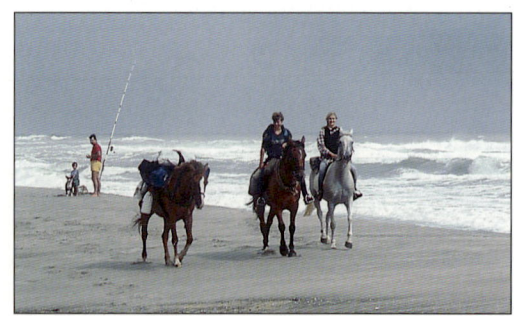
The Bay of Plenty coast

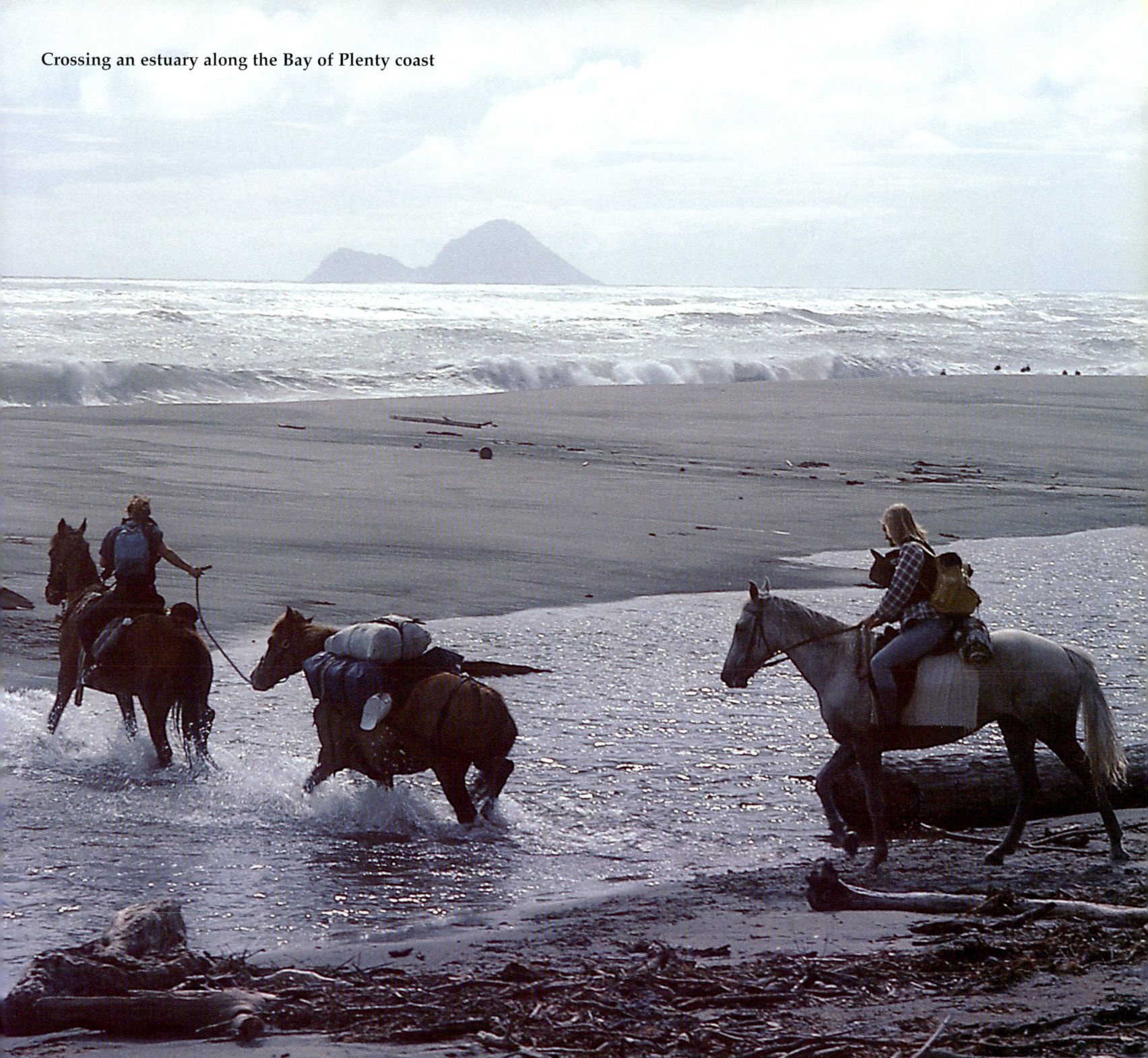
Crossing an estuary along the Bay of Plenty coast

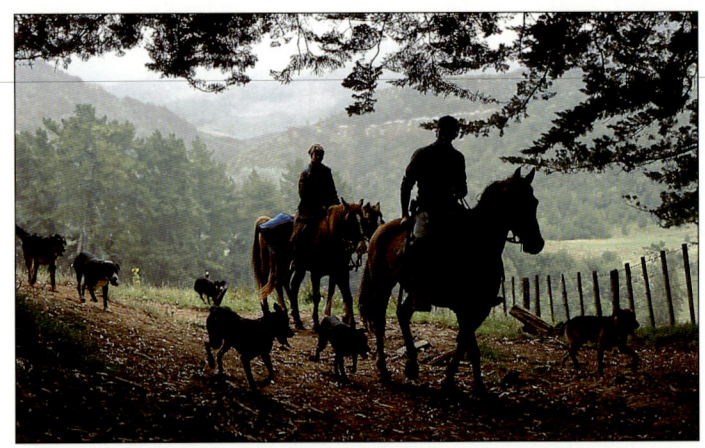

Dan Jex-Blake escorted us across Manapoike station and over the Wairoa river. The bridge had been lost in a cyclone which had also washed away a large proportion of the topsoil from the landscape.

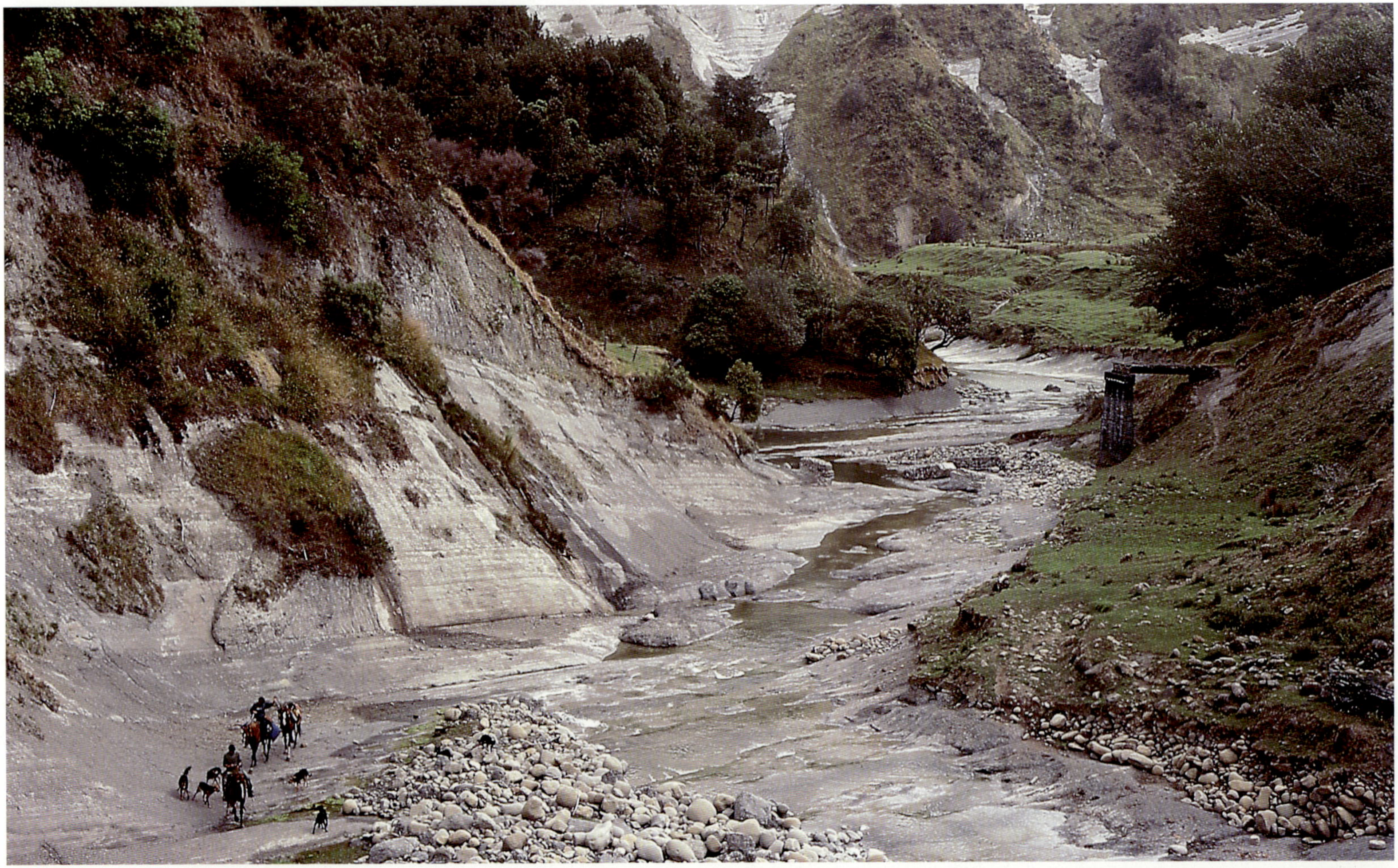

16
Waioeka Gorge

*Don't worry about anything, instead, pray about everything.
Tell God what you need.* Philippians 4:6 NLT

From Opotiki we headed south east through the noisy, bush clad Waioeka Gorge inhabited by trillions of clicking cicadas and numerous roaring waterfalls, plunging and crashing into the river which surged along the valley floor. We were confined to the one road leading through the gorge, and because of the traffic it was necessary to lead Monty. He was always very grumpy and stubborn when constricted by a lead rein and we took turns dragging him. He resisted, showing the white of his eyes in protest. To save our stretched out aching arms we experimented, tying the lead rope to Nelson's neck, but it got caught under his tail and he panicked, clamping his tail down trapping the rope. I tried to dismount but as Nelson and Monty twirled around we became more and more knotted together in the rope and I landed with a thud! After this episode we reverted to taking turns having our arms stretched and when there wasn't much traffic we let him loose. Cheerily he would trot on ahead in the middle of the road with his ears pricked, nonchalantly holding up any traffic which happened to come along, until we grabbed him to let the cars go by.

After the scuffle with the lead rope we were dismayed to see Nelson limping, so we prayed over his leg and continued, taking turns riding Roman and walking on our blistered feet out of the humid damp gorge.

We emerged into what looked like another country. A scorched dry landscape unfolded before us like a wavy brown carpet, eastwards towards Poverty Bay. It hit us forcefully that along with the rain, we had left the good grazing behind and were entering the East Coast drought. Our new challenge would be to find enough food for the horses.

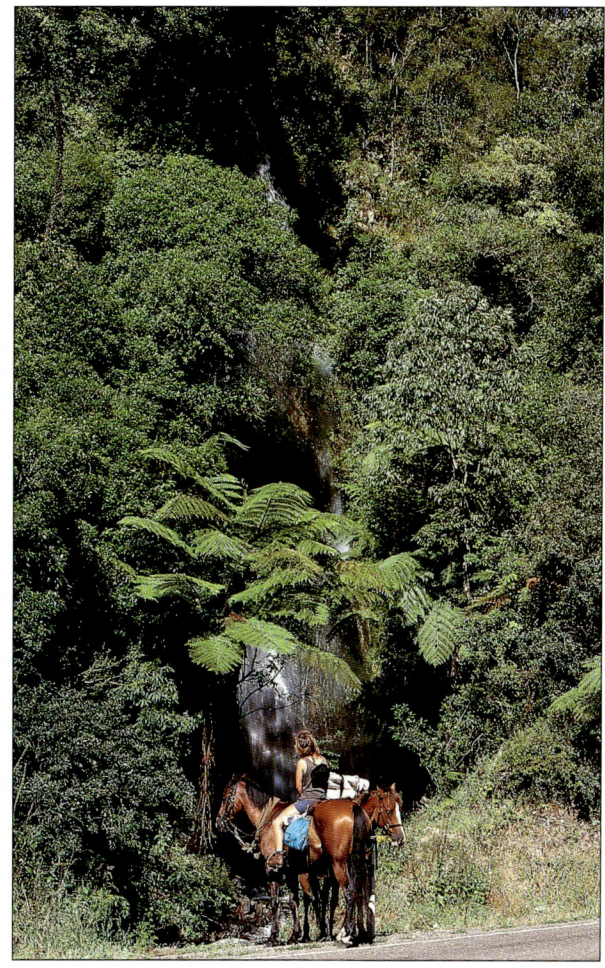

Ali, Nelson and Monty in the Waioeka Gorge

17
HAWKE'S BAY

Endurance develops strength of character in us.
Romans 5:4 NLT

In Gisborne we were put in contact with a polo-cross player, who could transport Nelson south with his horses to a match in Hastings, where we were planning to be in ten days time. This was the answer to our prayer. But it didn't prove to be easy!

Nelson was our lead horse and Monty and Roman stubbornly refused to go without him! Completely unperturbed at being left behind, Nelson nonchalantly grazed while we left in a flapping struggle. Jerkily stopping and starting, we inched our way forwards, south across a desert of dry and barren hillocks adjacent to the curved Hawke's Bay coastline. Now travelling at the hottest time of the year we left before dawn with the theory of avoiding the midday heat, but as progress was slow we were often still struggling in the hottest time of the day, coaxing Monty and Roman forwards, as neither of them wanted to go first. It was less effort to lead them on foot but we still had to drag them.

"It will be so good to have Nelson back!" I groaned, thinking of Nelson's easy swinging stride, as I pulled Roman who was refusing to proceed down a steep hill, "It really is a test of endurance without him!"

"You know, we are so far behind schedule on our visas, maybe we should exchange Roman for something faster!" Ali suggested, pulling on Monty's reins as he stretched out his head, stubbornly refusing to move.

"We can't afford another horse!" I stated the obvious and then added, "so we can trust God to get a good price for Roman and buy another!"

"Okay, let's!" Ali agreed, "as we'll never get to the Bluff at this speed!"

Having left our tent with the pack and Nelson, we slept wherever we could find a remnant of grass for our horses.

"Don't step on us guys, okay!" I told Roman and Monty, whose chewing was considerably amplified as they grazed around us while we lay on the ground in our sleeping bags looking up at a sky lit by sparkling stars.

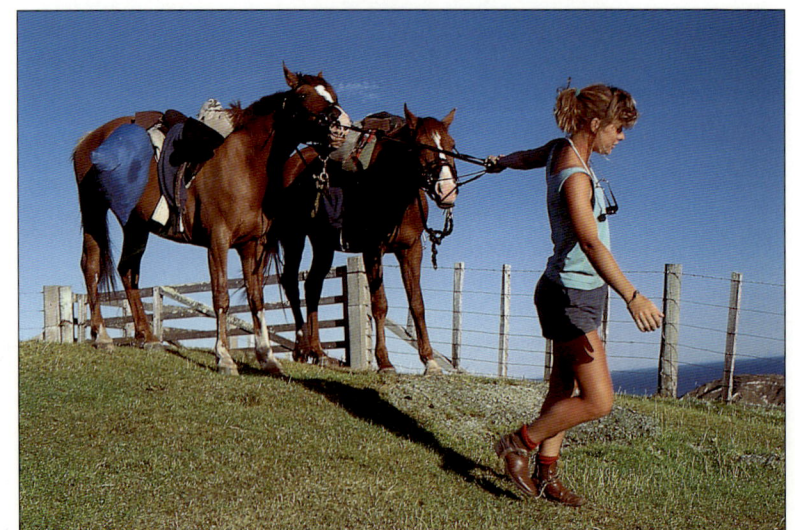

Monty and Roman refused to move without Nelson!

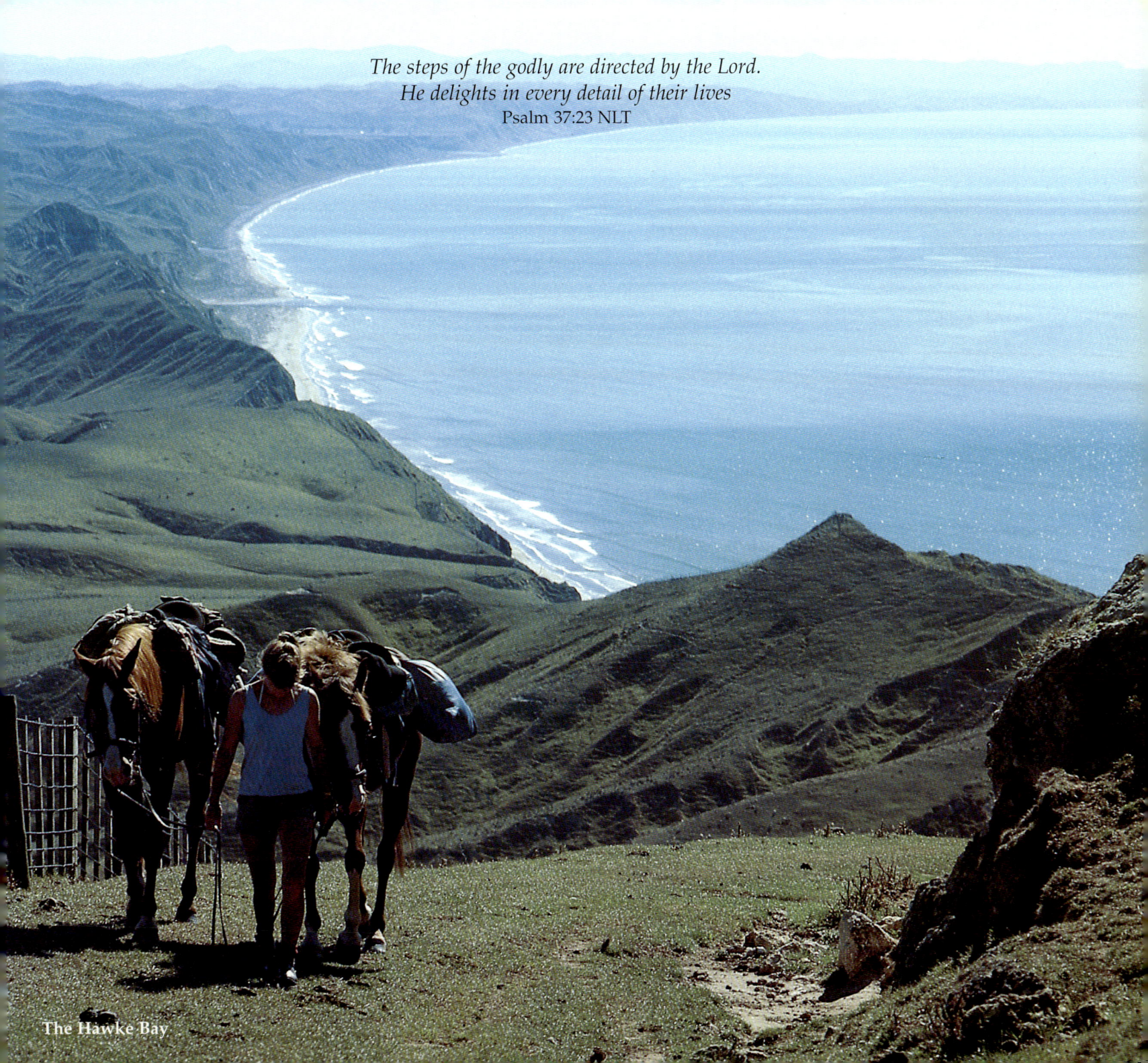

18
Honey

*Now glory be to God! By his mighty power at work within us,
he is able to accomplish infinitely more than we would ever dare to ask or hope.* Ephesians 3:20 NLT

At Waipukurau, where my sister Claire and her husband Ross McCormick farmed, we were all extremely pleased to be reunited with Nelson! Roman and Monty dashed up to him squealing with delight! Here, the horses gained the weight they had lost with three square meals a day and a good rest.

It was mid-February. We were now two months behind schedule, with only another three months extension on our visas and we weren't even half way. We visited the local Hawke's Bay M.P. hoping that he could help us with the visa authorities.

"I doubt very much you will get another extension and be able to finish your trek," he said solemnly as he showed us out, adding, "But, I will put it forward and maybe your God will give you another miracle!"

We had to gain time and although we had grown very fond of Roman, struggling with him over 600 miles, he wasn't getting any faster. Hearing of our predicament Claire had acquired an old mare from a neighbouring station.

"You don't have to take her!" She impressed, "she's never been off the station in her life and was destined for the meat man but he never showed up. I know she sounds a bit dubious but try her out anyway!"

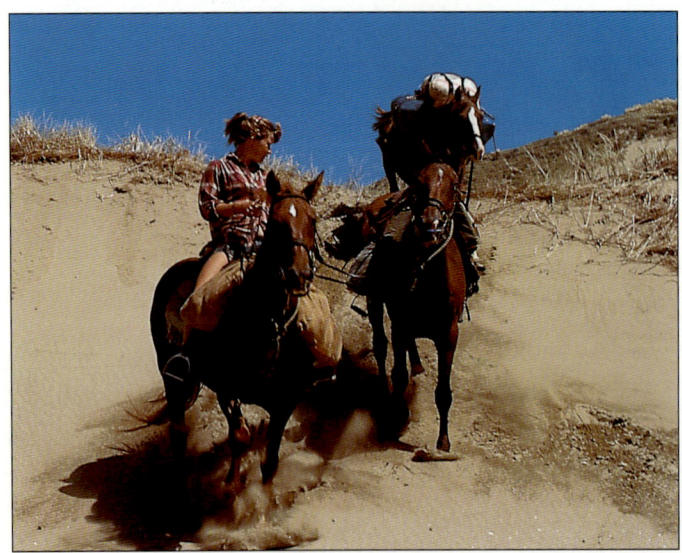

Ali on Honey, followed by Nelson and Monty

Her name was Honey. She was a small 14 hand stocky chestnut mare and although she hadn't been ridden for five years she went everywhere we directed her, fast! We sold Roman to a lady who wanted a quiet hack, she offered $550 for him but when she came to collect him paid $600! This gave us finance to continue and also buy Honey for the asking price of NZ$70 (£25, less than one fifth of the amount we paid for each of the other horses.) She proved to be the most suitable of all the horses for our tough expedition and was as fit as the rest of us within two weeks!

"Wow, God is so good, hey Trace?" Ali exclaimed with a sigh as she once again sat astride Nelson, enjoying his swinging stride as Monty jogged at his side.

"Oh, He sure is!" I agreed and gave Honey a pat on her neck. She seemed to know she had been reprieved from the meat-man and never having left the farm in her life she stepped out with her ears pricked and a spring in her step, eager to see the rest of New Zealand!

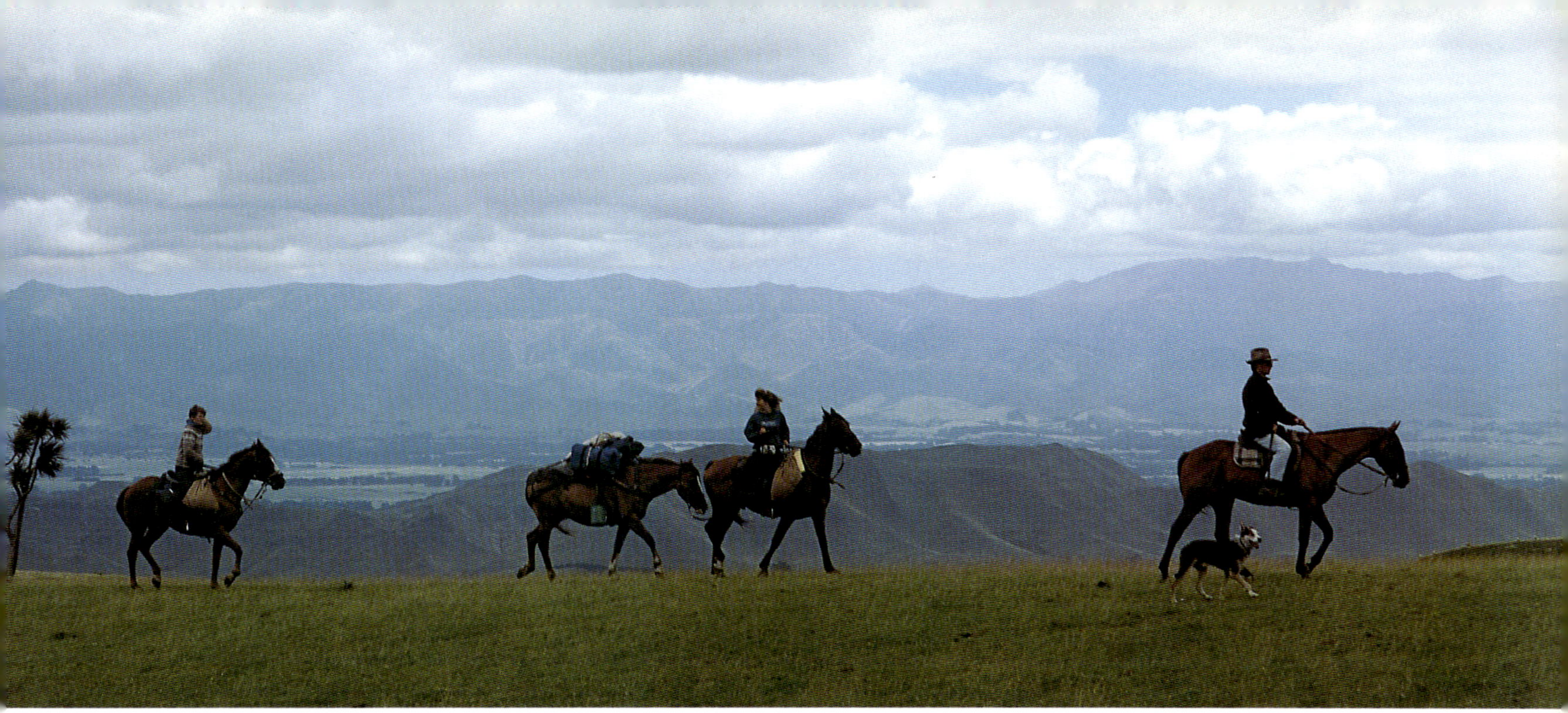

With the Ruahine Range as a backdrop Ross McCormick leads the way over Waitomo farm followed by Ali and Claire.

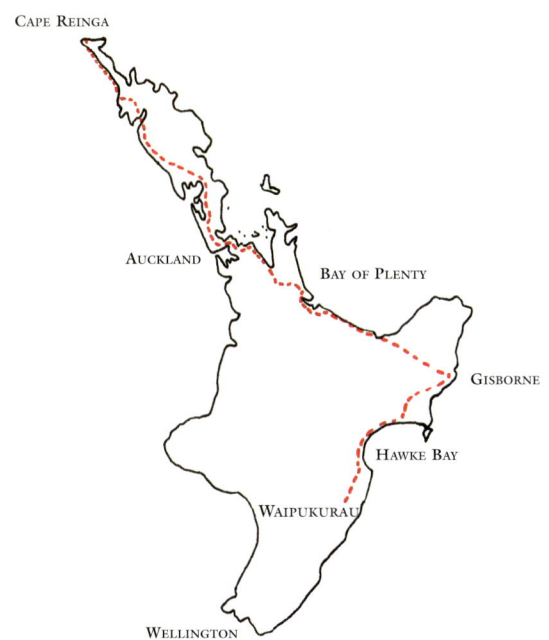

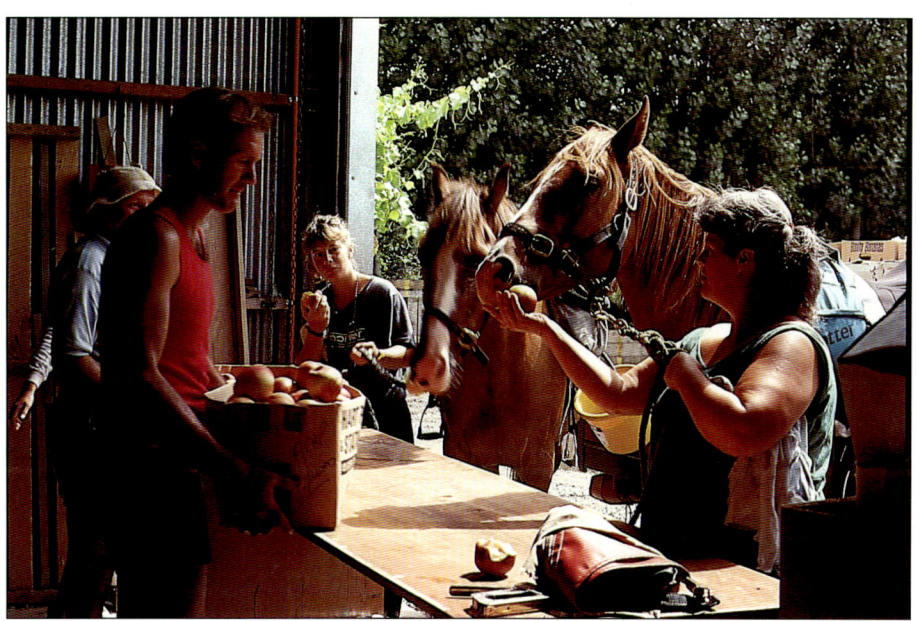

In Hawke's Bay province we dropped in to see our old fruit picking gang.

19
Losing things

Why worry about clothing? Your Father in heaven knows you need all these things
Matthew 6:28,32 GNB

Our packs lightened as we left a trail of our gear along the route. Our frequent back-tracking to find lost property made me feel like we were riding New Zealand twice in both directions! Lost items included the majority of our grooming kit, tethering ropes, horseshoes, clothes, coats, boots and bed rolls, so we had to get accustomed to sleeping on the hard ground! All these seemed inconsequential compared to the times when we lost our horses, resulting in frantic searches through the New Zealand countryside!

While riding barefoot along the Bay of Plenty coastline, twice I lost my riding boots which I had tied to my saddle. Once we went back and found them, the second time I thought one had been washed out to sea. Just as I was wondering if I would have to ride barefoot from then on, some boys ran after us, one of them holding my boot!

We overloaded the saddle 'D' attachments, so they continually broke away from the saddle and we kept having them repaired.

Riding along the Wairarapa Coast the wind blew Ali's hat into the sea. Impulsively, I dashed in to rescue it and a large wave washed over me. Wet and triumphant about retrieving the hat I realised I had lost my watch, but then time didn't really mean much to us anyway!

On another scorching day, after rummaging through the whole pack several times, I discovered I had lost my only pair of shorts. I was melting in my dark blue riding trousers until later that day I found a pair of shorts on the road right in front of me and they were just my size!

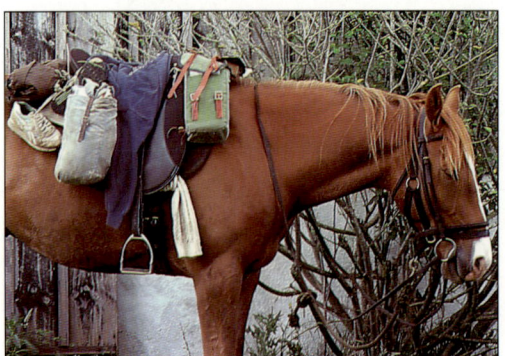
All loaded up!

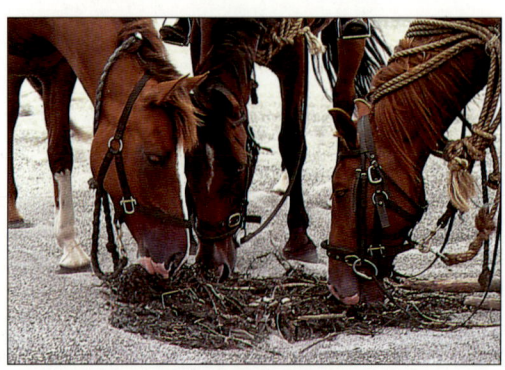
Checking out whether the seaweed was edible!

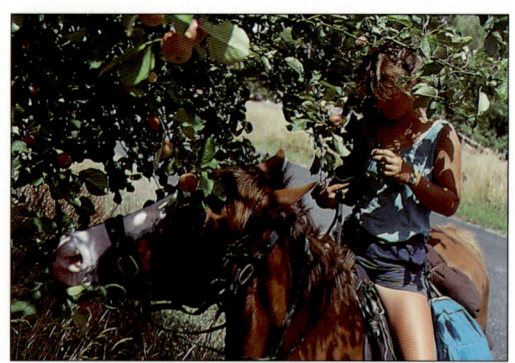
Ali and Monty apple picking!

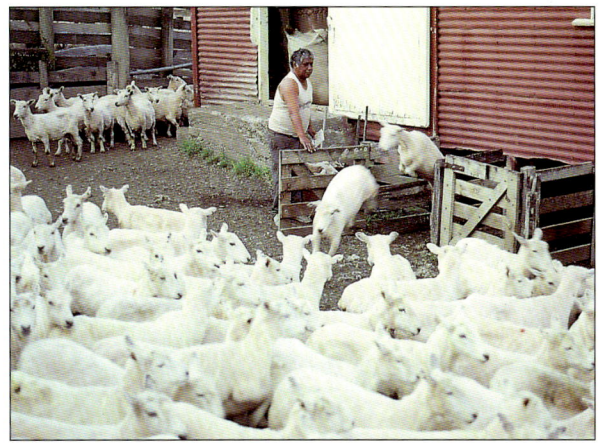 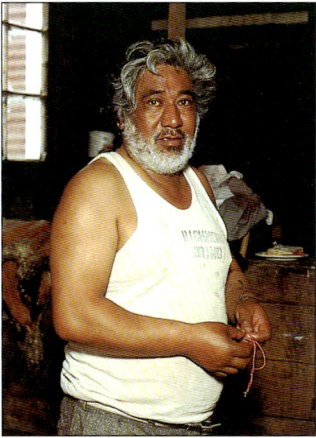 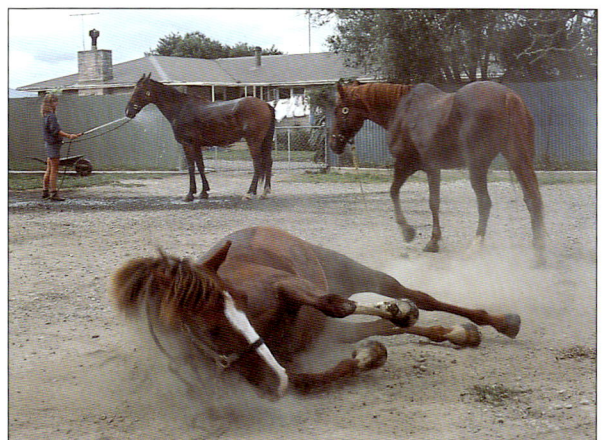

Above & right: Shearing time at Waitomo and Tip Kiri Kiri

Monty rolling after being washed down!

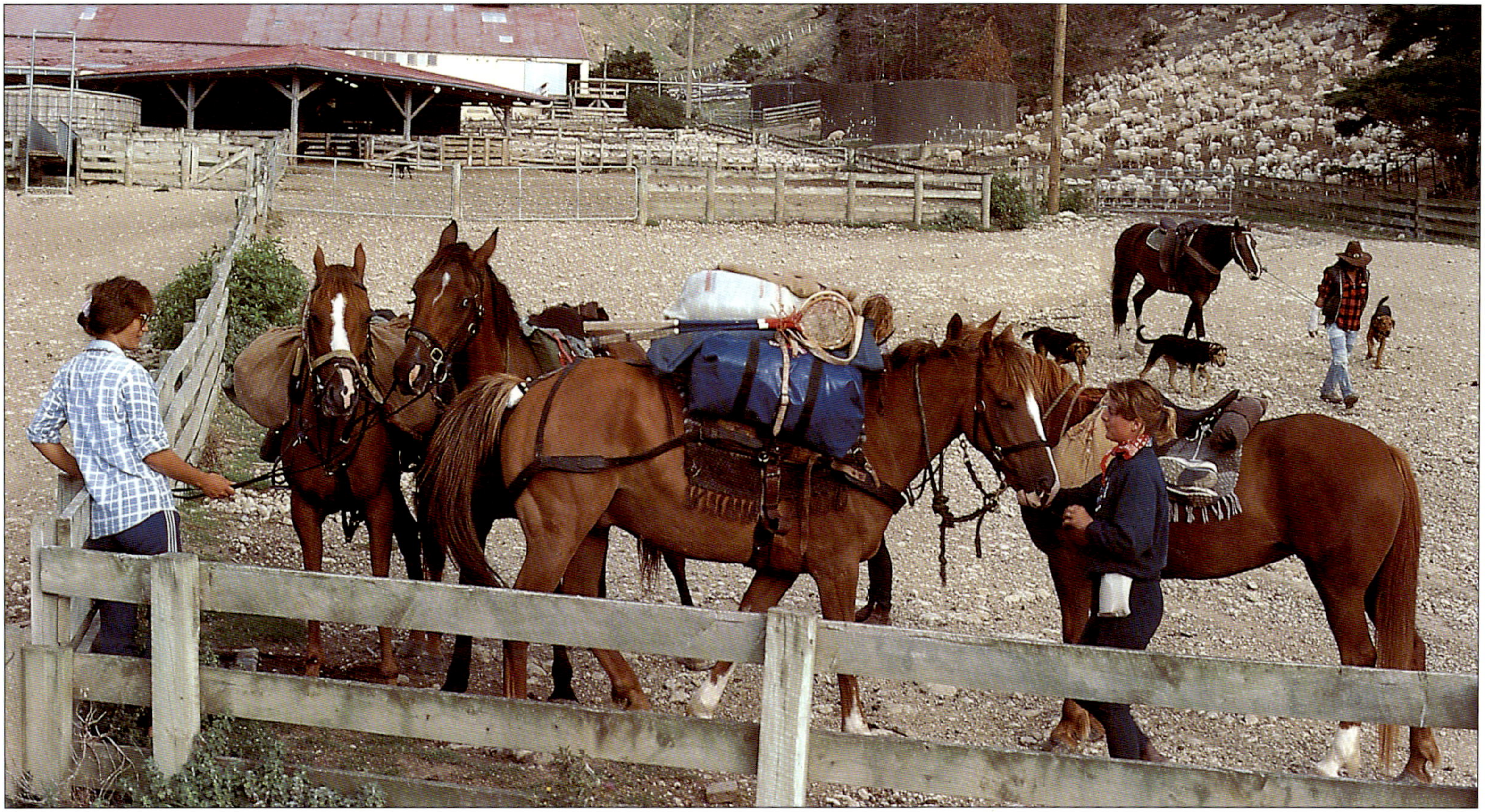

Kathy Flemming and Claire McCormick with the horses at Owahanga Station.

20
FACTOR 15!

For the Lord God is a sun and shield; No good thing will He withhold from those who walk uprightly.
Psalm 84:11 NKJ

As the whole of the East Coast of New Zealand, including the Wairarapa, was suffering a serious drought, we carried as much grain as possible in pekau sacks tied across our horses withers. These continually shifted from side-to-side until we ran out altogether. The people on the remote Wairarapa coast were especially hospitable and invited us in, fed us roast mutton and generously gave our horses their valuable hay.

Sam Hunt, the famous New Zealand poet, incongruous in tight black jeans, sunglasses and a voluminous white shirt met us with great gusto and gesticulating extravagantly, began rhapsodising some verses about our horses. Then he invited us into his corrugated dome-shaped abode for a beer and a smoke, which we politely declined.

"Well, if you won't have a green smoke have a green note!" he rhymed, and handed Ali twenty dollars, adding "For the cause!"

The intensive sun and persistent wind whipping off the Pacific, which dried the coastal vegetation brown, also sun dried our faces to a leathery texture. We applied our precious Elizabeth Arden factor 15 sun cream to Monty's pink nose, which blistered in the sun. Not appreciating our gesture of concern, he immediately wiped his nose on us, or across one of the other horses!

He also hungrily ate Ali's straw hat, which I had rescued from the sea and finding that tasty, he then surreptitiously sidled up beside Honey and grabbed mine, which was tied to my saddle to prevent it blowing away. A struggle ensued and I got my hat back but it was never quite so elegant again, with a big bite taken out of the rim!

As we rounded Cape Palliser we tied up our horses while we went to take a closer look at a colony of seals basking in the sun. Disgusted by their pungent odour, our horses untied themselves and headed on at a brisk walk. We had to run to catch up with them!

At Lake Ferry, to save a whole day's journey around the Lake we swam the horses across the estuary and skirted the Turakirae Head towards Wellington. On route Monty, unabashed, introduced himself to a large group of people with dreadlocks and tattoos heading in the opposite direction. They stopped to give Monty Christmas cake and apples and asked us if we had seen any grass.

"There's hardly a blade up the whole coast!" I replied thinking how our horses would love some green grass while Ali lent over and nudged me, "Trace, I don't think they mean that sort of grass!"

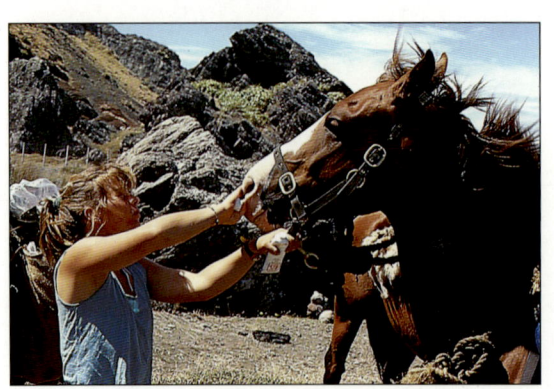

Ali applying factor 15 sunscreen to Monty's nose!

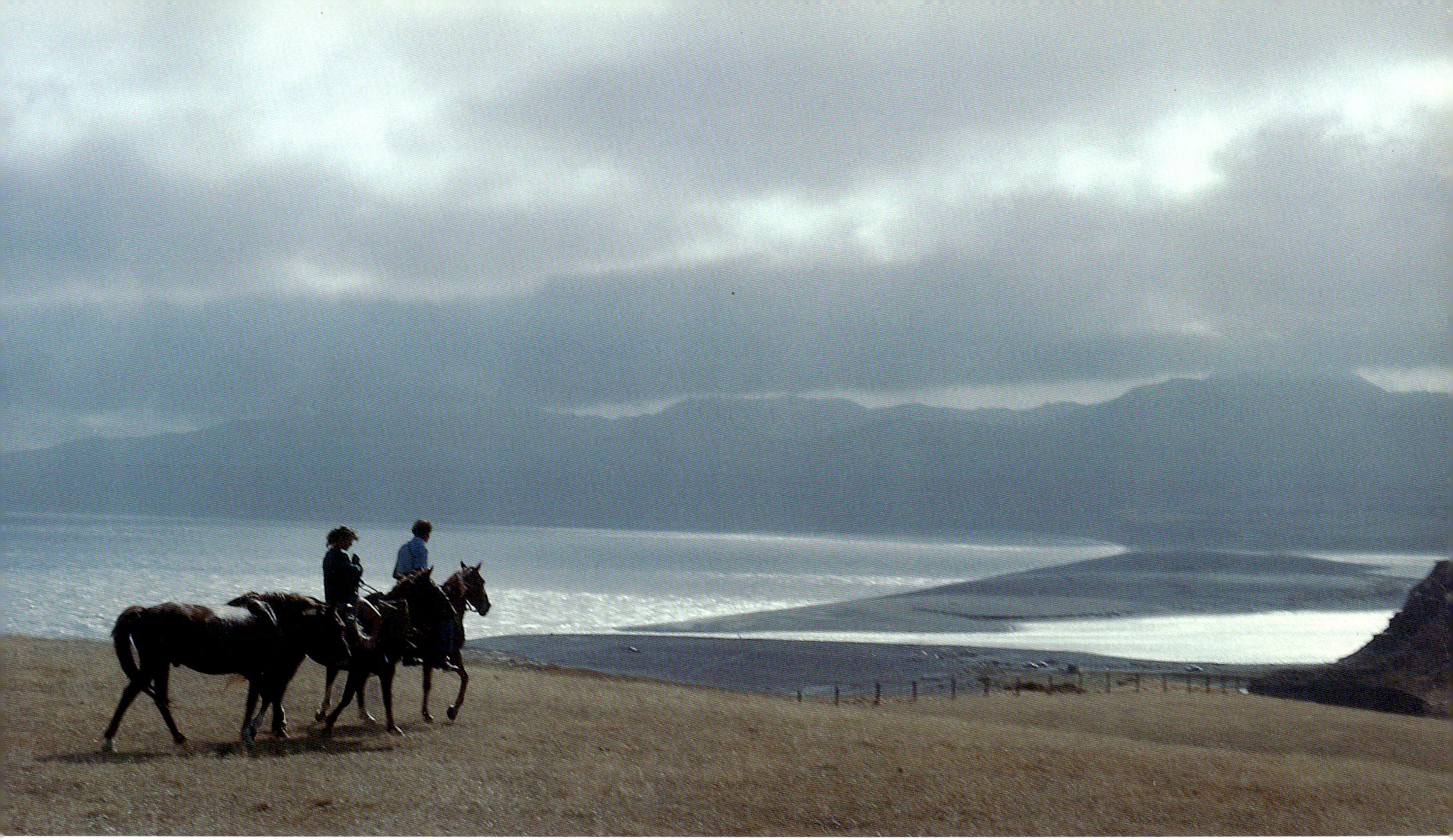

Donald McStraith guided us down to Lake Ferry where we swam the horses across the estuary

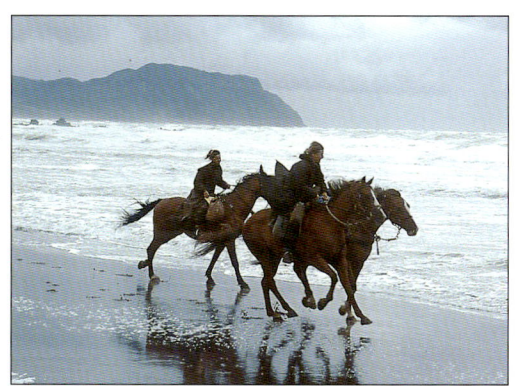
Claire and Ali cantering along the Wairarapa

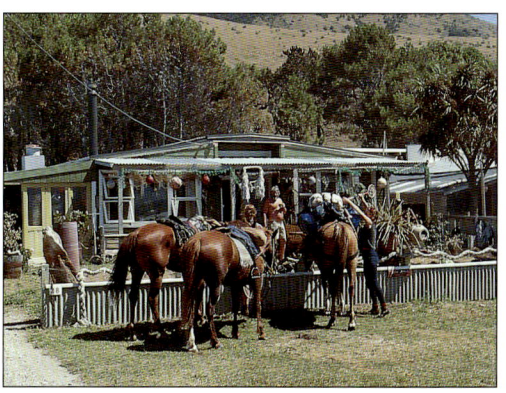
Invited to lunch on the Wairarapa

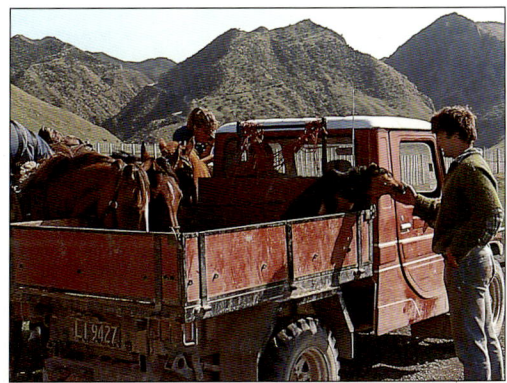
Monty and Nelson checking for food!

21
WELLINGTON

Blessed shall you be in the country and blessed shall you be in the city
Deuteronomy 28:3 NKJ

Wellington, the capital of New Zealand, was a shock after the remote Wairarapa coast where the people were so relaxed and hospitable. The only approach into the centre of the city was along the Hutt motorway, a narrow corridor sandwiched between the sea and railway on one side and sheer hills on the other.

Our horses shied violently away from the frequent commuter trains into the dangerous oncoming traffic, drivers blasting their horns. Adding to this nightmare we could barely see the road ahead as a deluge of rain was falling and the passing vehicles sprayed us with water.

Drenched to the skin, we rode down Lambton Quay, the main street of the capital, lined with towering buildings. This was a shocking introduction to city life for Honey, who had never before been off the station. With a look of amazement in her eyes, her neck like a giraffe, she stuck close to Nelson and Monty, who were by now much more experienced, but still got agitated with the traffic.

While our horses were occupied munching hay on the verge of the main street in the city centre, we collected for Tearfund as vehicles manoeuvred around us.

Our bedraggled party caught quite a lot of attention in the middle of the city and as smartly dressed businessmen and women marched by they dropped offerings into our bucket which was also filling up with rain water. One bus driver, stopping at the lights dropped a $5 note into our bucket while some office girls threw some change out of a second floor window and another brought us a welcome cup of hot coffee. While a road sweeper skirting around us, our scattered hay and horse droppings, mumbled;

"I'm not paid to clear up that you know."

Our long arduous day fund-raising in Wellington produced record takings of over $1000 for Tearfund and the Bangladesh flood victims but was almost lost when Monty broke the handle of the bucket and we scrabbled to recover the hundreds of coins rolling across the road! Much worse, in the Capital we lost our horses again!

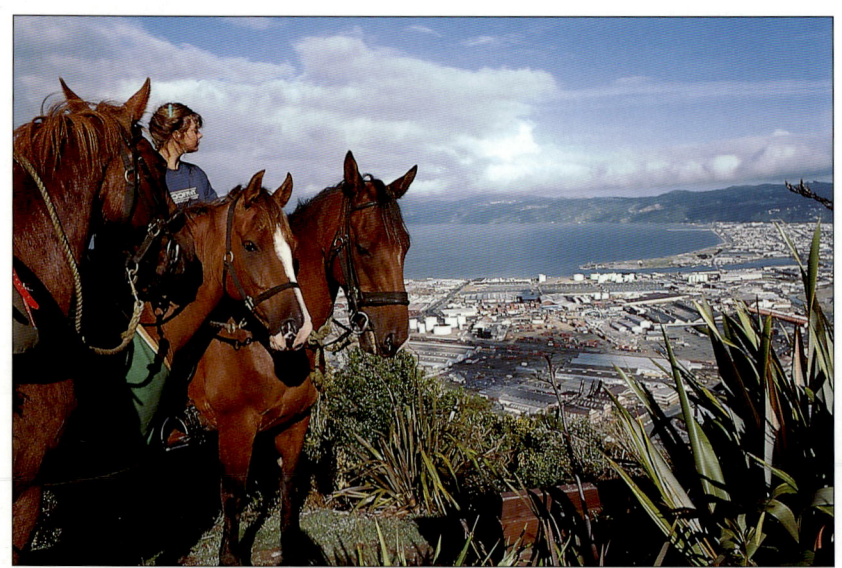

Overlooking Upper Hutt on our way into Wellington.

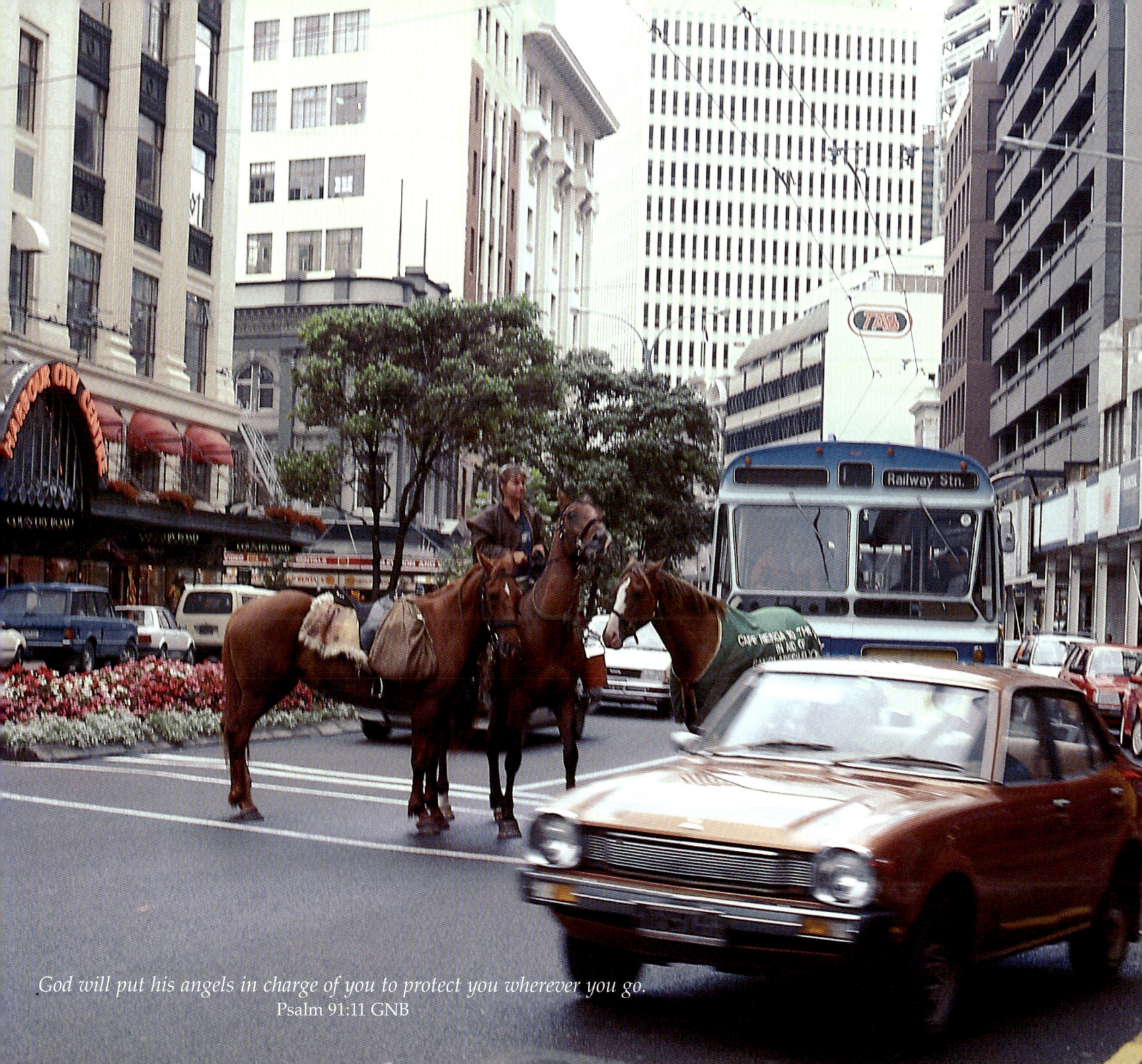

God will put his angels in charge of you to protect you wherever you go.
Psalm 91:11 GNB

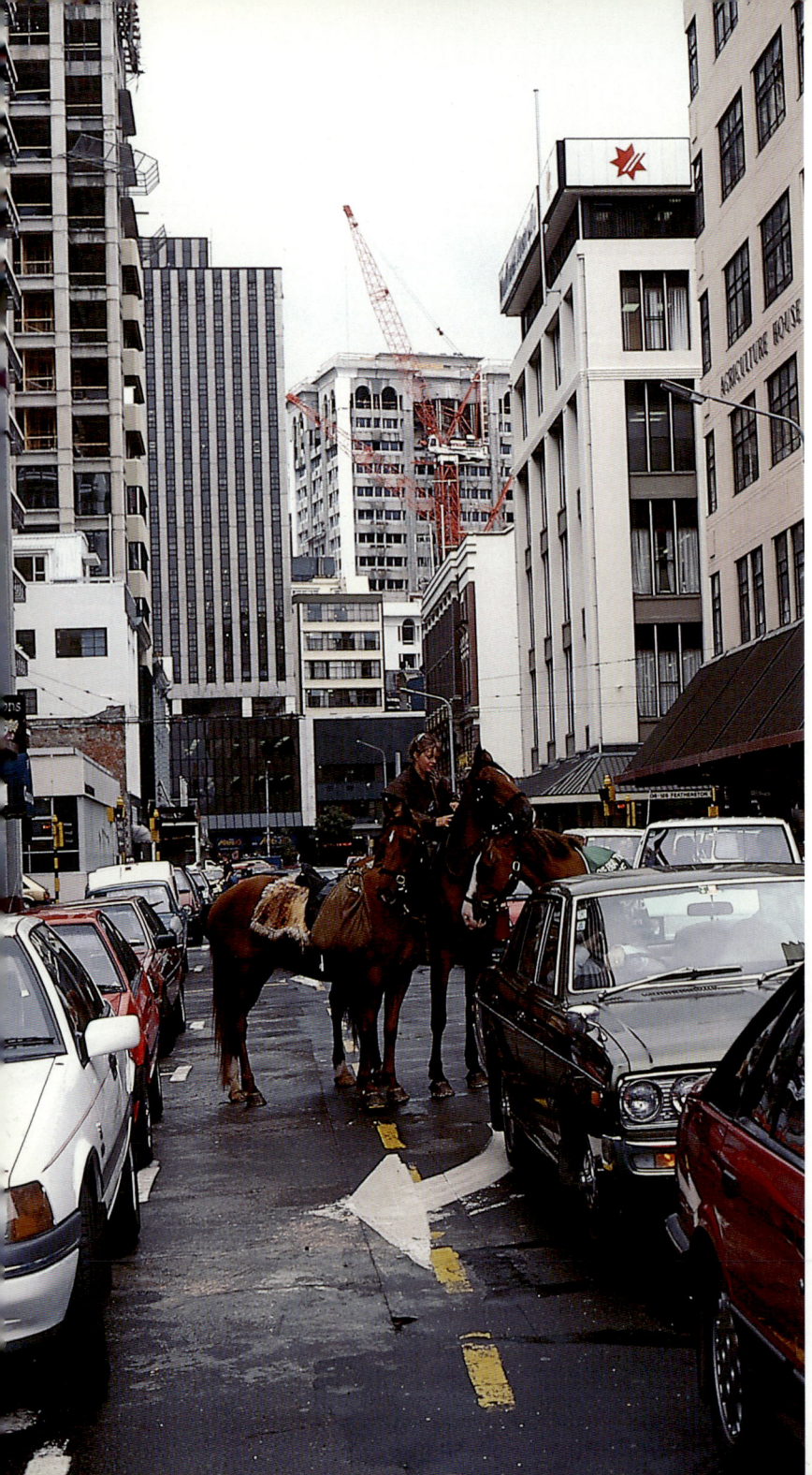

22
Lost in the Capital

The young lions lack and suffer hunger;
But those who seek the Lord shall not lack any good thing.
Psalm 34:10 NKJ

For over a week we had been trying to secure a free passage across Cook Strait to the South Island because we couldn't afford the expensive fare for our horses. Our visa time was ticking away and we seemed stuck in the Capital.

Restless, obviously bored with city life like the rest of us, Nelson, Monty and Honey escaped their paddock one night and early the following morning we were rushing down the streets asking anyone if they had seen some horses!

We found them at the top of a terraced garden feasting in the vegetable patch!

"Just get them out of here!" An hysterical woman dressed in a deep pink night robe with matching slippers shrieked from the safety of her back door step, as though they were wild animals from Africa!

Hastily we led Honey and Nelson down the narrow winding steps while Monty with his usual bravado launched himself off the top terrace. Plunging his hooves into the lawn below, he ducked under the washing line and then sprang off the next terrace landing with all four legs spread eagled creating sparks and skid marks across the tarmac! Then, with a nonchalant look on his face he looked over his shoulder to see us making a more careful descent as if to say,

"Hurry up, you lot, let's go!"

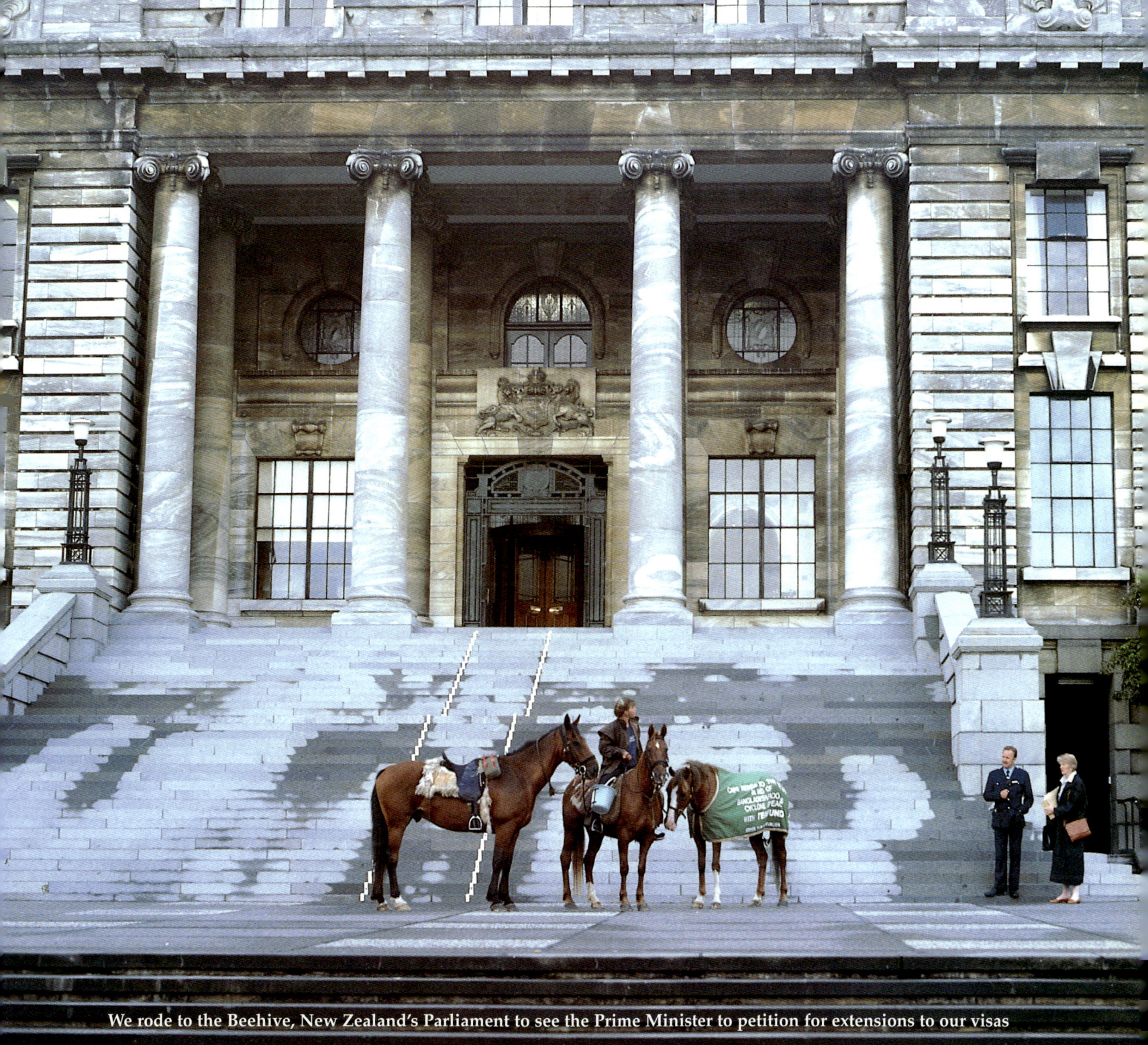

We rode to the Beehive, New Zealand's Parliament to see the Prime Minister to petition for extensions to our visas

23
WAITING ON THE QUAY

Trust in the Lord with all your heart, and lean not on your own understanding;
In all your ways acknowledge Him, and He shall direct your paths. Proverbs 3:5 NKJ

We were all restless and impatient to get going to the South Island, as we had been in Wellington over ten days. In that time we had ridden up to the Beehive, the houses of Parliament, to personally petition the Prime Minister.

We were informed by the M.P. we had seen in Hawke's Bay that the Prime Minister was away and,

"I don't have any news on your visa applications."

"But we need an extension soon!" Ali implored, "We've only got another month to ride the whole length of the South Island!"

"Otherwise," I added, " we'll be outlaws on horseback!"

"I'll follow it up," he replied in a matter-of-fact way, before turning and retracing his steps into the Beehive.

We had tried every solution to get over to the South Island. We contacted the ferry company, the railways, and numerous livestock transporters.

"Sorry," we were told, " this is one of the most expensive stretches of water in the world, we usually take race horses." Rather faint-hearted we took it back to the Lord in prayer, believing He had the solution.

"Be at the ferry terminal at 6.45 this evening and tell my driver I said you could go with him!" Neil Pilcher from Inter-Island Horse Transport said to Ali and she let out a squeal of delight.

Thanking God, we leapt into action as we only had a few hours to get there. At such short notice we couldn't find anyone to transport us down the dangerous Hutt Motorway to the ferry terminal. Even the traffic cop couldn't help. He explained it was rush hour and they were too busy giving motorists speeding tickets! So once again, with our complete trust in God's protection we charged down the motorway pressing our horses on at a fast trot, the more we pushed them the less they shied at the passing trains into the oncoming traffic. With sweat dripping from their flaring nostrils and heaving flanks we arrived at the terminal with great relief.

"We don't see many horses turn up in this fashion!" remarked a group of dock workers, as they gathered around and supplied a bucket of water to wash our horses down.

The time to embark arrived but there was no sign of the Inter-Island truck. As dusk darkened to night and the other vehicles were almost loaded, it became alarmingly obvious that we might be left alone, all night, marooned with three horses on a concrete quay in the city.

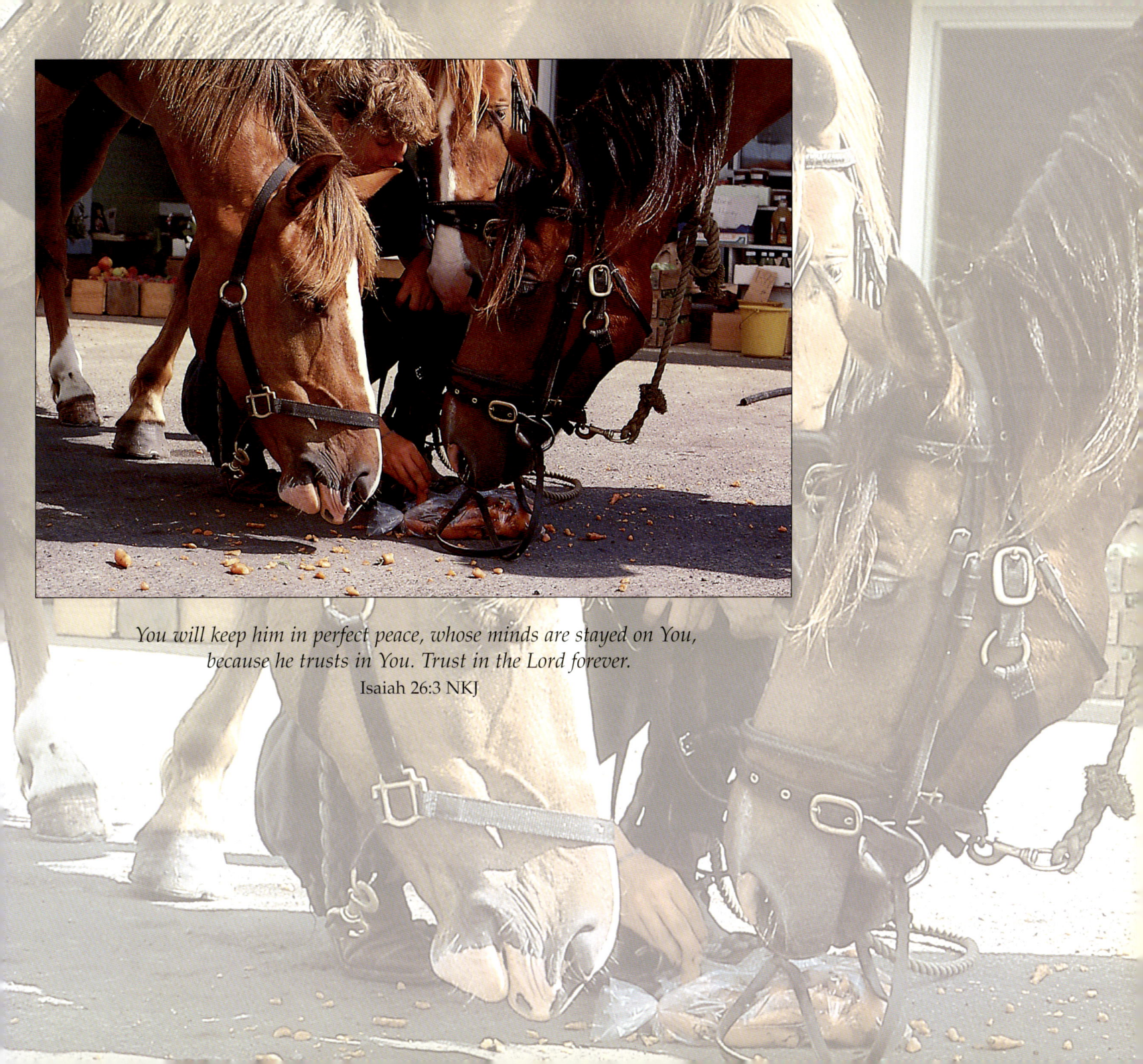

You will keep him in perfect peace, whose minds are stayed on You, because he trusts in You. Trust in the Lord forever.
Isaiah 26:3 NKJ

24
COOK STRAIT

We know that all things work together for good to those who love God, to those who are called according to His purpose. Romans 8:28 NKJ

The last few cars rumbled on to the ferry as an elongated truck with blazing headlights swung hurriedly on to the quay. Ali, throwing me Monty's reins, dashed over to it.

"Neil, your boss said we could come with you!" she gasped - before the driver, jumping down from the cab, had touched the ground.

"Is that right?" he replied in surprise. "Well, how many horses have you got?"

"Three!"

"Well, someone up there must be looking after you!" He looked heavenward and continued, "I should have had only two spaces but because I was running late I didn't have time to pick up a horse so I have space for your three! Let's get them loaded quick, otherwise we'll all miss the ferry!"

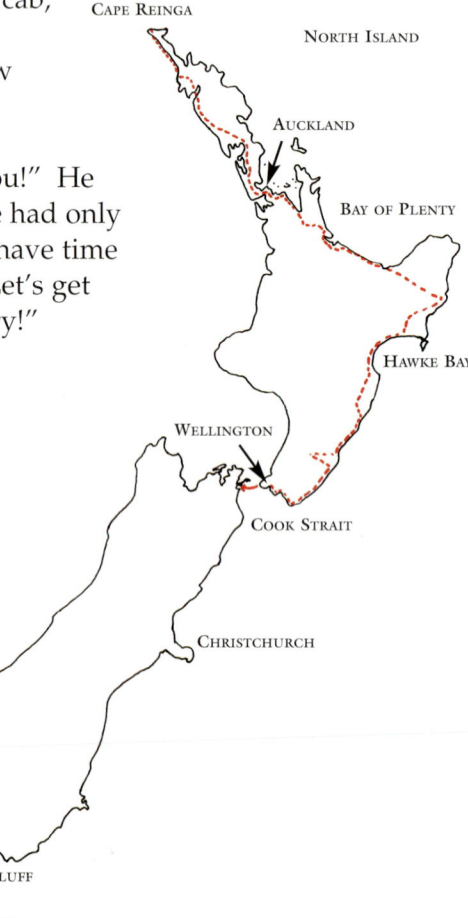

Cook Strait

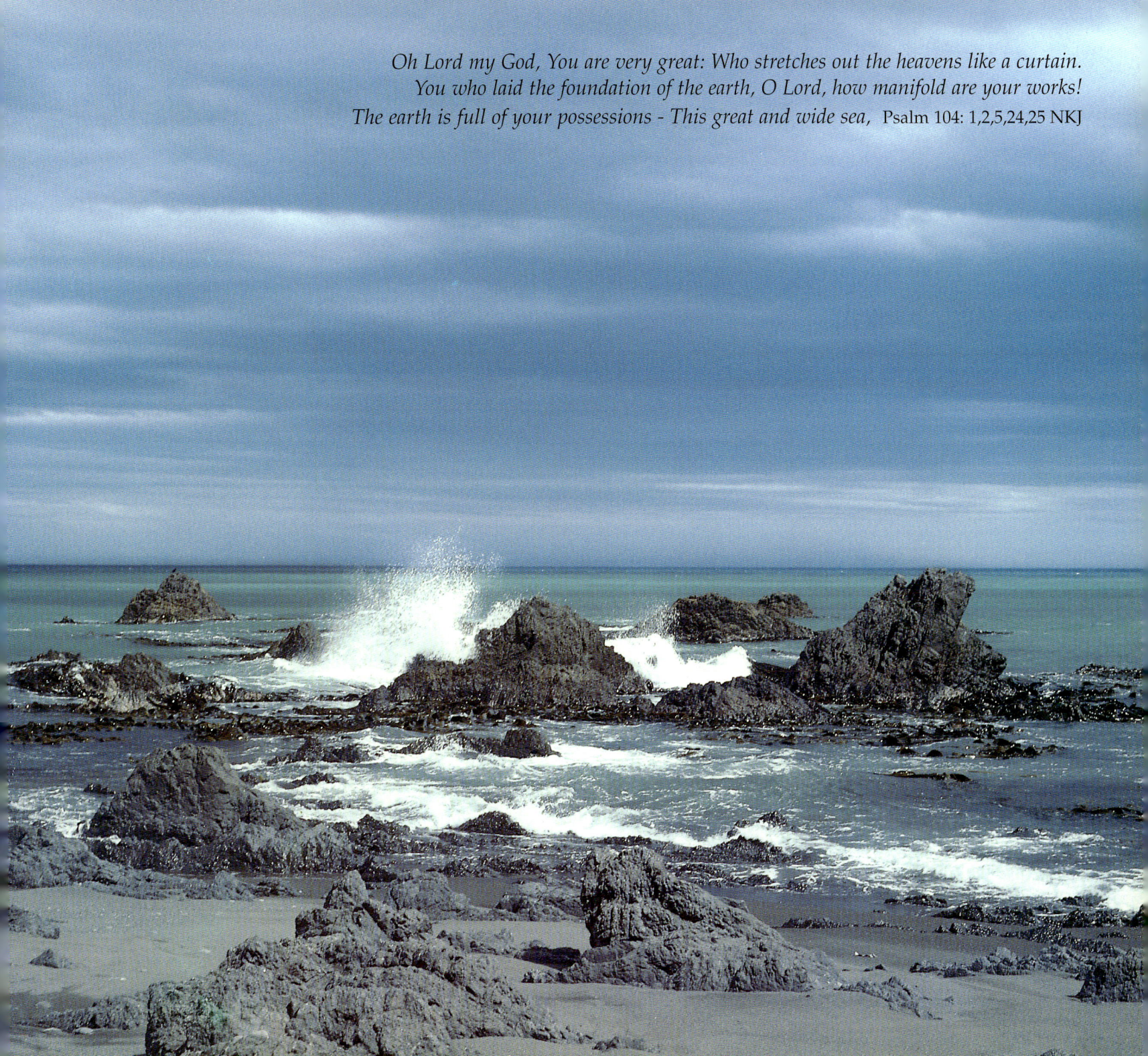

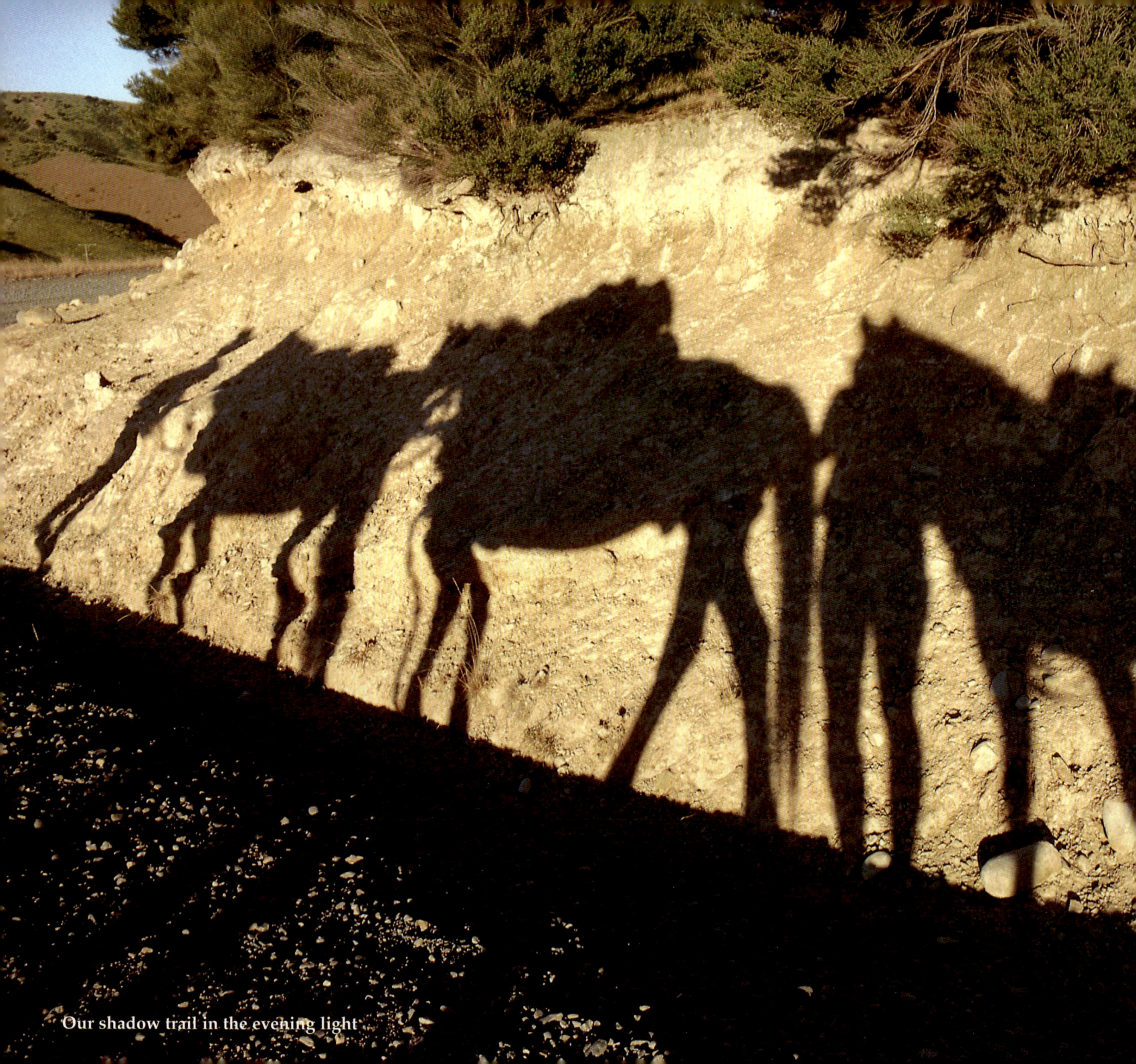
Our shadow trail in the evening light

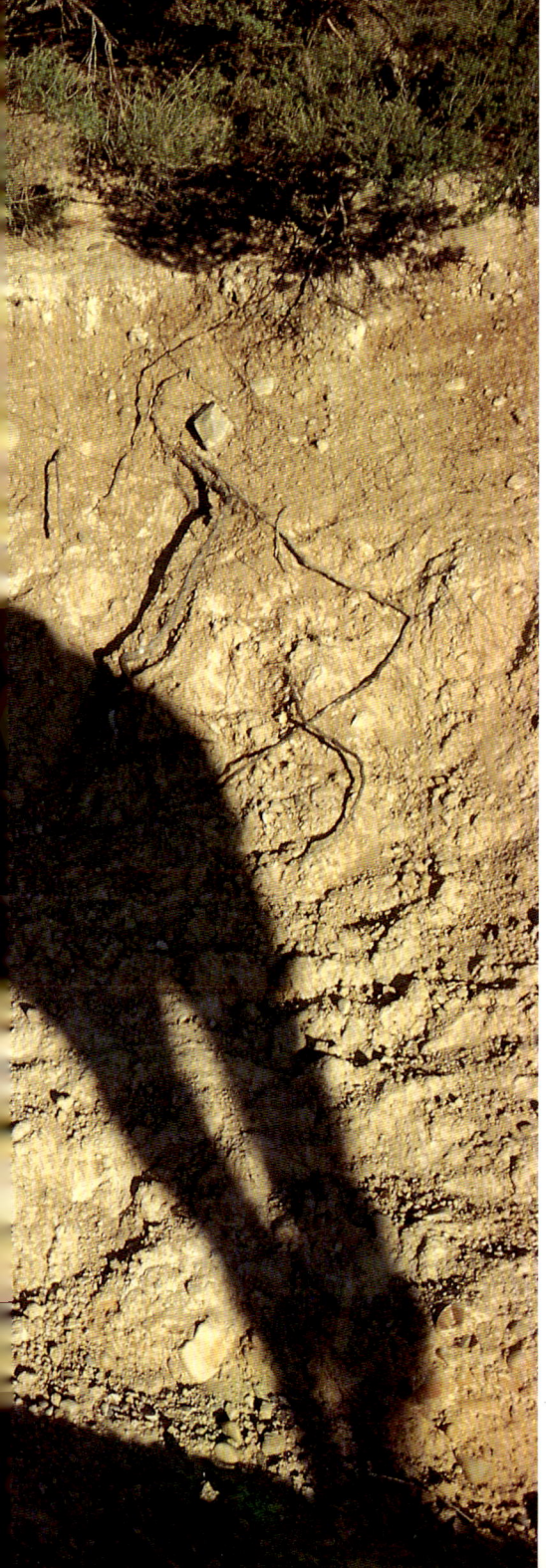

25
THE SOUTH ISLAND

His mercies are new every morning. Great is His faithfulness
Lamentations 3:23 NKJ

As we watched the city lights of Wellington and their reflections in the harbour water diminish into the night, we thanked God for His great faithfulness and I felt a rising excitement to be bound for the South Island of New Zealand.

When the Polynesian seafarers arrived in New Zealand more than a thousand years ago they found the South Island cold and rugged. In 1642 Abel Tasman described it in his journal 'A large land uplifted high', but he was prevented from landing because of the hostile Maoris and it wasn't until 128 years later, in 1770 that Captain Cook landed in New Zealand.

It was nearly midnight when we disembarked at Picton in the South Island and knocked on the door belonging to a Pastor, Lester Terril and his wife, Judith. Lester, dressed in pyjamas popped his grinning face out of the bedroom window and offered to help make an enclosure for our horses which took several hours and consisted of our tethering ropes knotted together, propped up by poles. Although they had plenty of good grass to graze, the security wasn't convincing and I was mindful of their two previous escapades!

In my sleep I heard the hooves of escaping horses.

"Quick Ali, the horses are out!" I said urgently as I shot out of my sleeping bag and jammed on my boots. Together we charged down the steep garden. As I shone the torch around our make shift enclosure, our resting horses blinked at the dazzling light and I could hear them say,

"Do you have to shine that torch right in our faces and wake us up in the middle of the night?"

"Sorry guys, sorry Ali, I must have dreamt it!" I apologised and we returned up the hill to our beds at a much slower pace. But the next morning my dream became a reality as the horses, refreshed after their rest, had decided to have a look around town!

26
Molesworth

*I will both lie down in peace and sleep;
for You alone, O Lord make me dwell in safety.*
Psalm 4:8 NKJ

The Terril boys sitting on Monty, Honey and Nelson

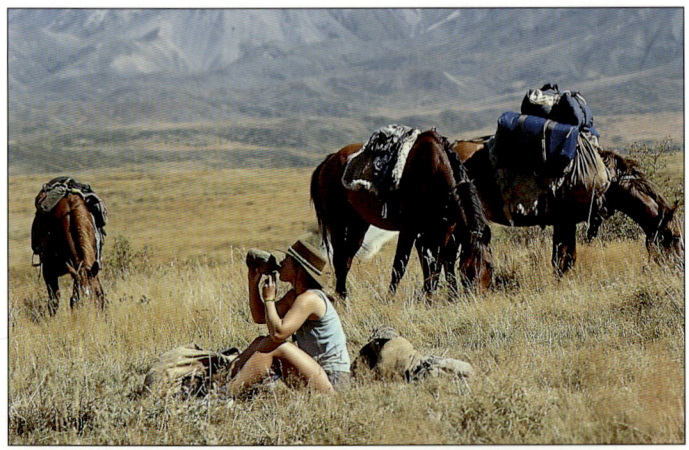
Ali having a drink and rest on Molesworth

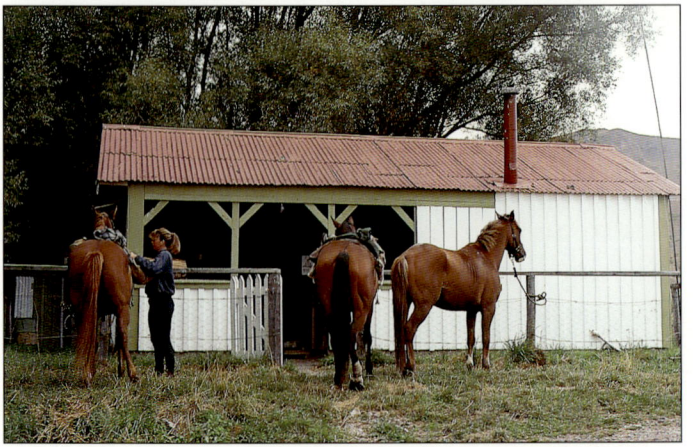
Ali saddling up Honey outside the Molesworth hut

After catching up with our horses, we saddled up and left the pretty harbour town of Picton. It was mid-March, the beginning of autumn in the Southern hemisphere and the air was freshly spiced with the aroma of pine trees which cloaked the surrounding hills.

We camped on stony ground in our little two-man tent, as we pushed inland, through strong winds, towards the Southern Alps, the backbone of the South Island. These High Country stations in the South were much larger than those we had ridden over in the North. Tussock grass, planted by the wind, was the only plentiful crop, along with the plague of rabbits. This serious pest, introduced by the British at the turn of the century, now erode the countryside and consume thousands of stock units worth of grass. However the Merino sheep, originating from Spain and once being one of the most lucrative forms of farming in New Zealand, also thrive in the High Country.

Riding across Molesworth, the largest station in New Zealand consisting of half-a-million acres and covering an area of 700 square miles, we slept in a shepherd's hut in the middle of a howling, windswept plain. Several people had recounted haunted happenings in this hut and these whirled around our minds like the wind around the hut. The flickering candlelight and glowing fire cast elongated shadows across the walls and ceiling as we wrote our diaries. As I climbed into my sleeping bag, I prayed and wedged in my earplugs, determined that nothing spooky was going to disturb me!

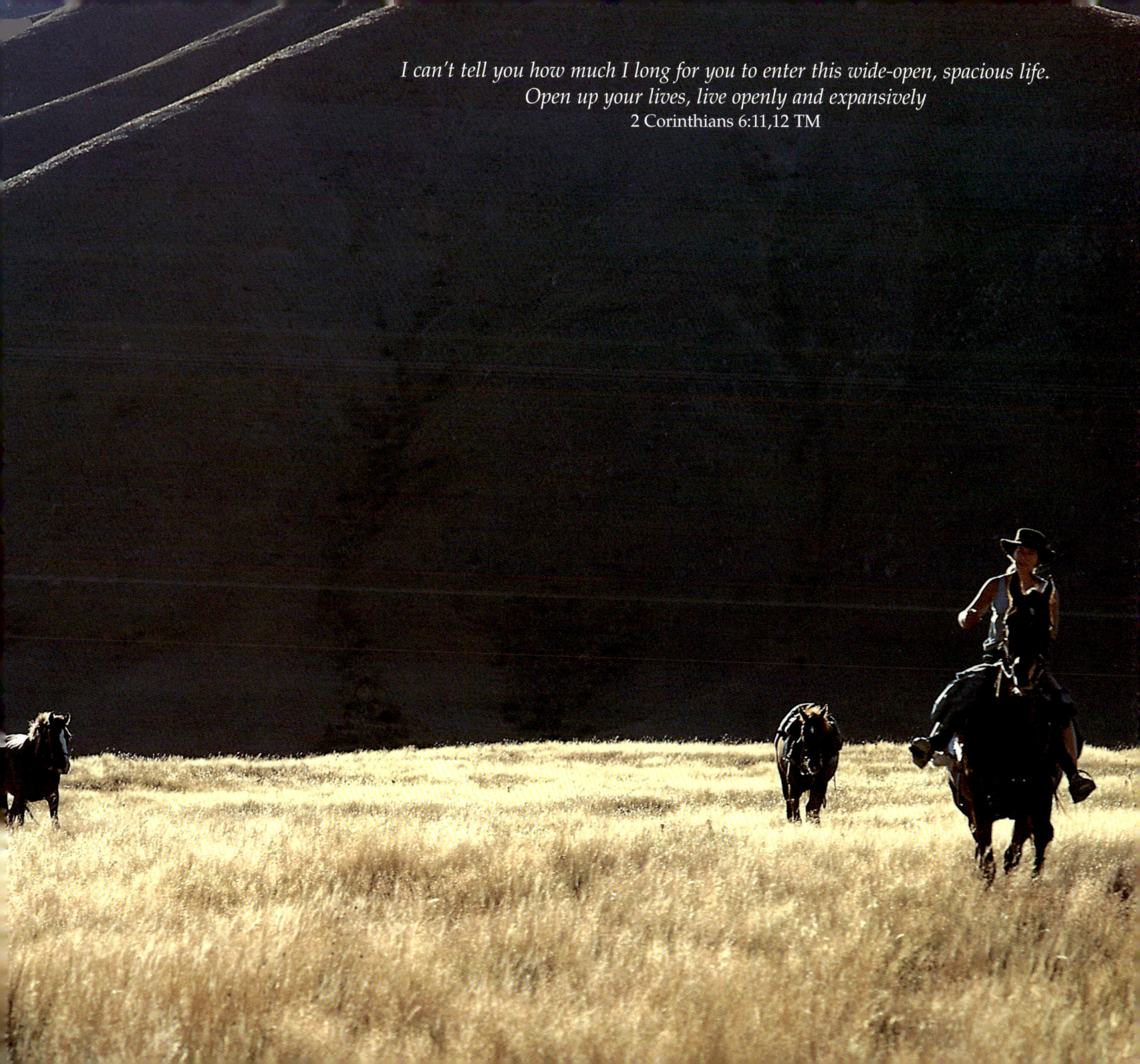

*I can't tell you how much I long for you to enter this wide-open, spacious life.
Open up your lives, live openly and expansively*
2 Corinthians 6:11,12 TM

27
JOLLIES PASS

Along unfamiliar paths I will guide them; I will turn the darkness into light before them and make the rough places smooth. Isaiah 42:16 NIV

I was relieved when I woke up and it was light!

I was still in my Snoopy T-shirt when a truck pulled up outside. We were scrambling into our clothes when there was a loud knock on the door.

"I'll take your packs on to the springs if you're quick!" offered the stocky and weathered manager of Molesworth, much to the relief of our tired horses. In an average day we would cover twenty-five miles but that day, as our pack and camping gear had gone on ahead we had to push on to cover forty.

It was a long, hard day trotting over rocky ground but we eventually reached Jollies Pass. The sinking sun was casting its last rays across the golden plains of Hanmer, spreading out below us, encircled by a rim of hillocks shadowed in relief.

Then the sun dropped behind the mountains and we descended into a dense forest and once again we were lost in the dark!

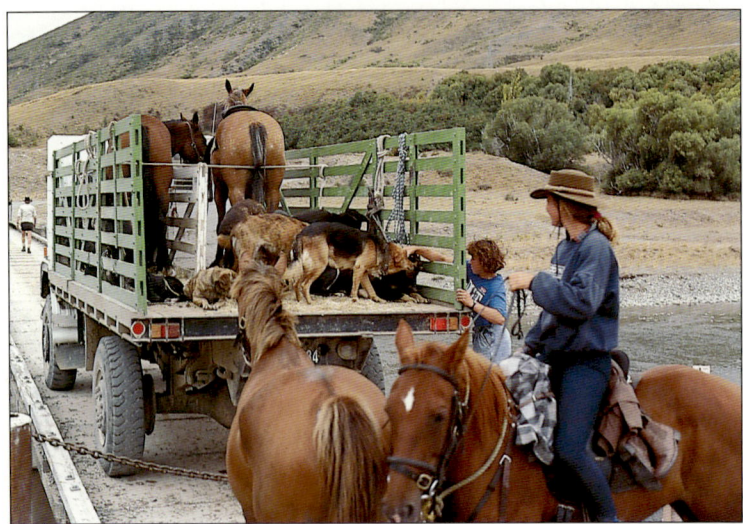
Meeting the Molesworth truck heading in the opposite direction.

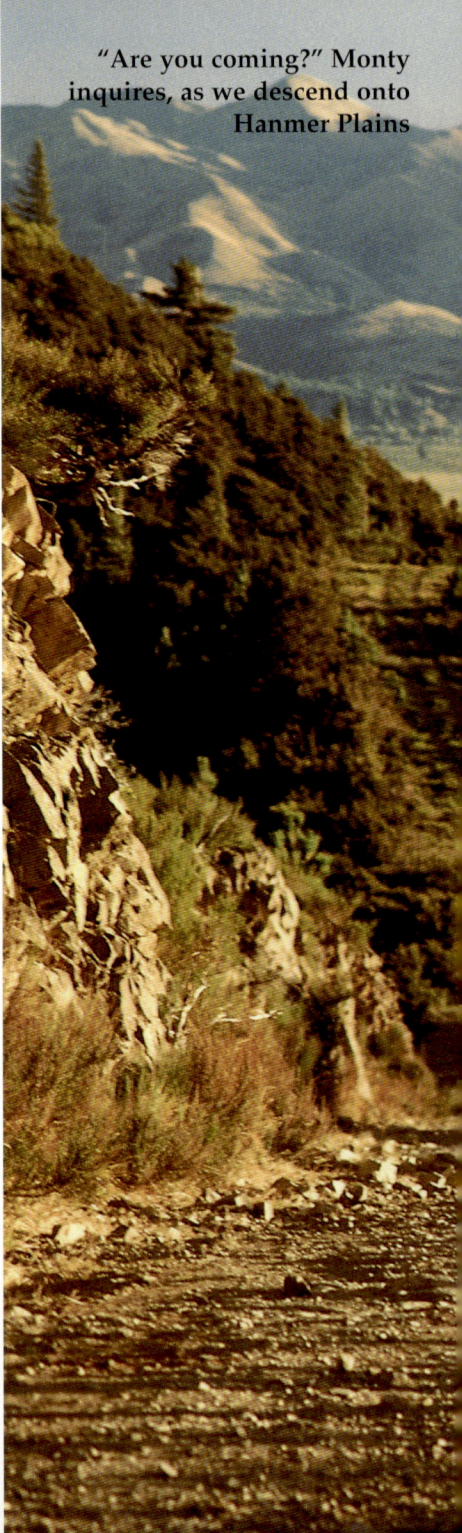
"Are you coming?" Monty inquires, as we descend onto Hanmer Plains

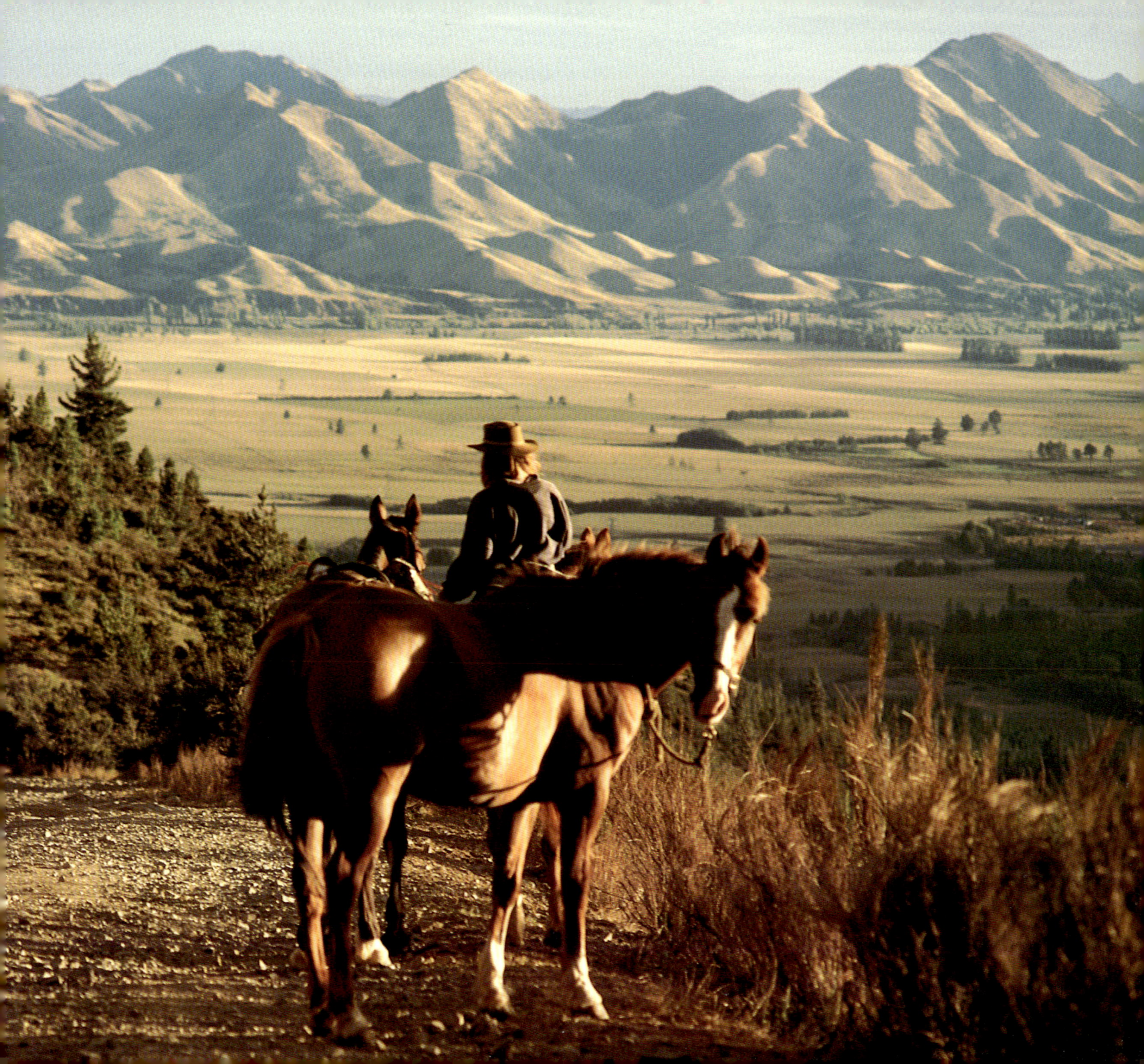

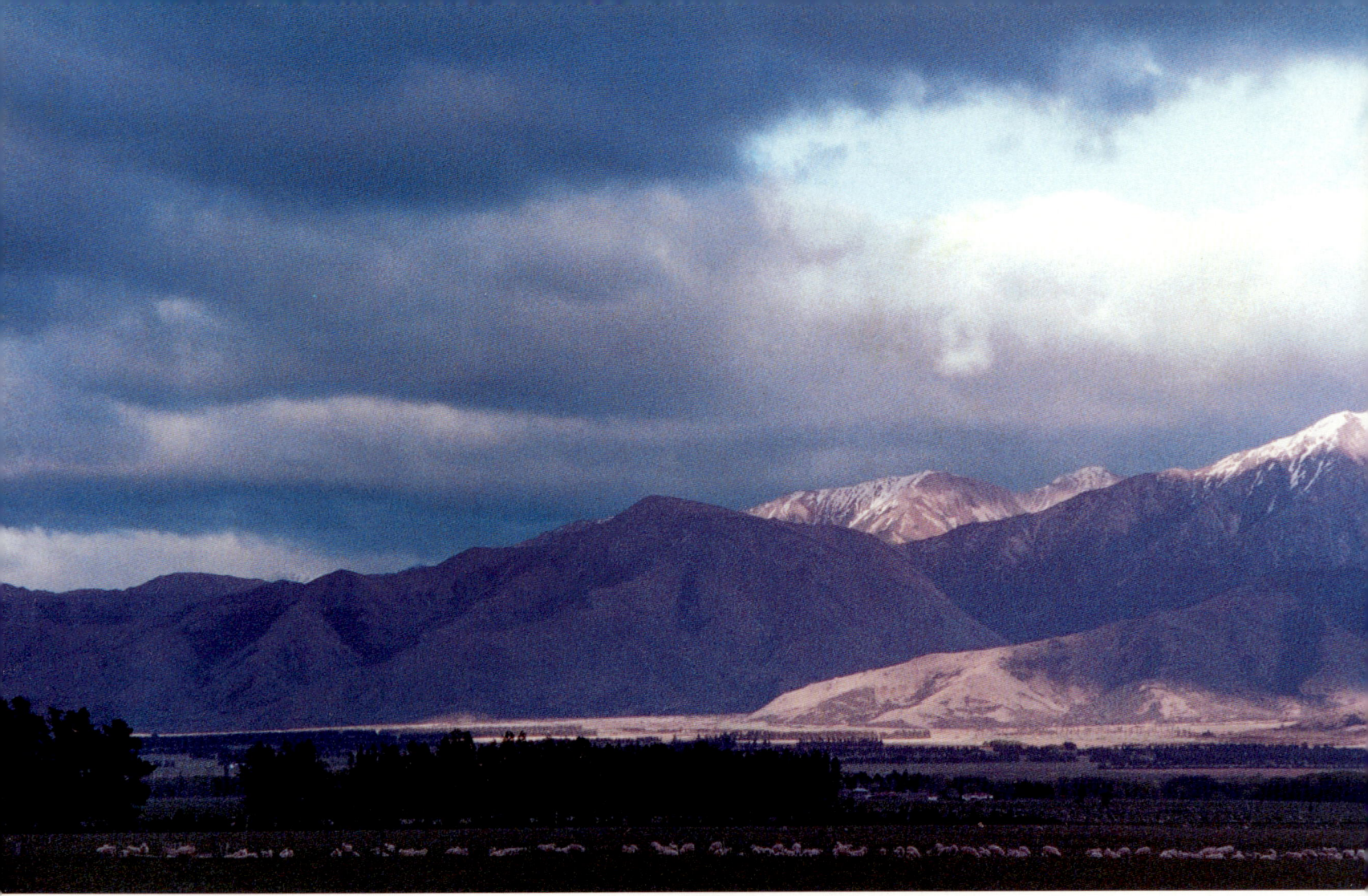

28
HANMER SPRINGS

Ali had made a contact in Hanmer Springs and had a few scribbled notes on how to get to their farm, but we couldn't read them in the dark as our torch had preceded us in our pack! So in a quandary, we kept riding following a road through a thick forest, hoping for a flash of inspiration as to which turning we should take!

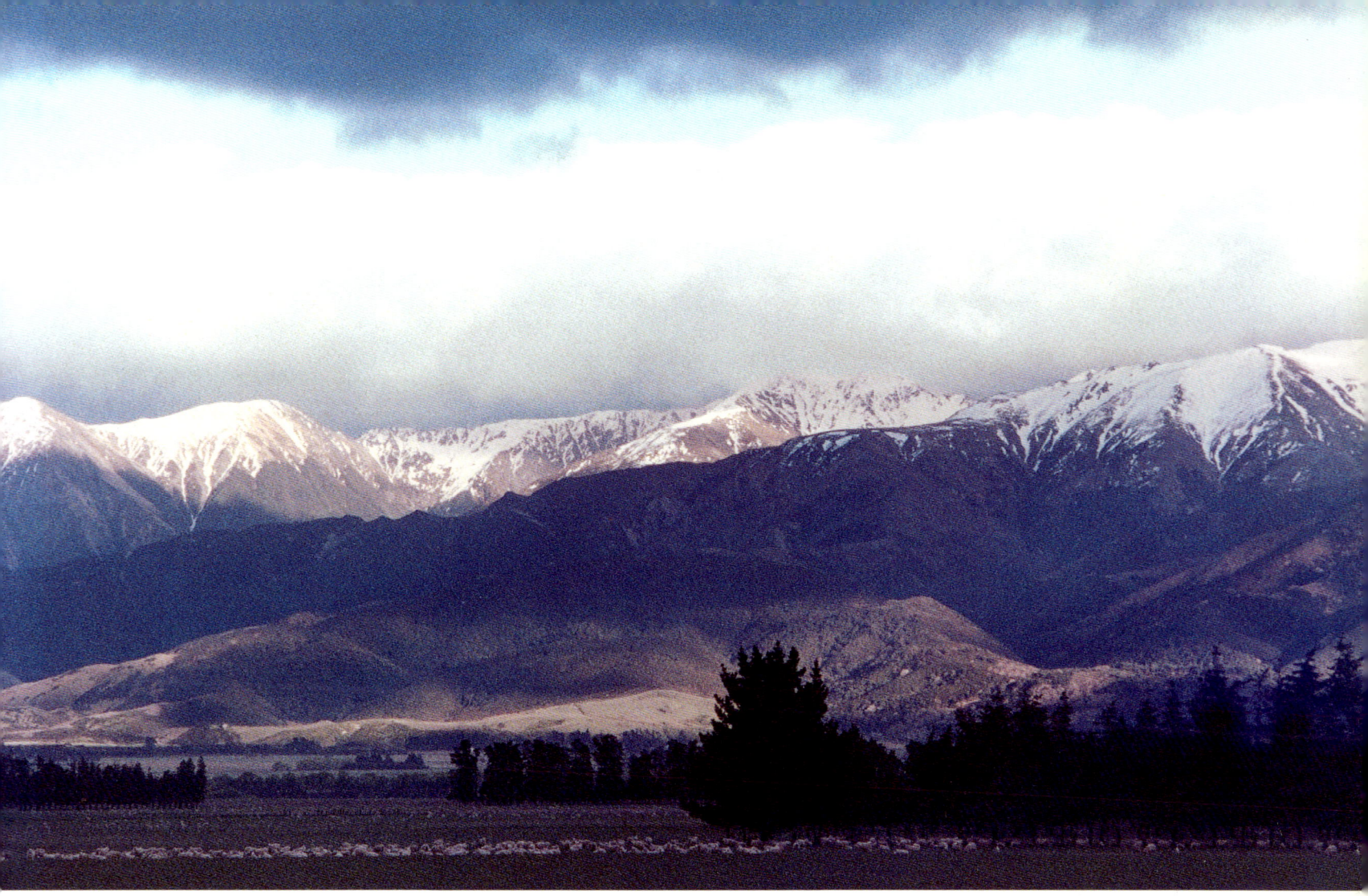

Hanmer Plains; where we all rested at Ross and Moira Long's farm

"Let's take a break and get a little rest". Mark 6:31 TM

Headlights from an approaching vehicle dazzled us and a dark figure called, " Is either of you Ali?" We introduced ourselves to Moira and Fiona Long, Ali's contact, and followed their vehicle through the forest maze to their farm where we rested for several days and prepared for our expedition over Harper Pass.

29
HARPER PASS

The steps of a good man are directed by the Lord.
He delights in each step they take. If they fall it isn't fatal,
for the Lord hold them with his hand.
Psalm 37:23,24 TLB

Ali and Wayne heading up the Hurunui valley

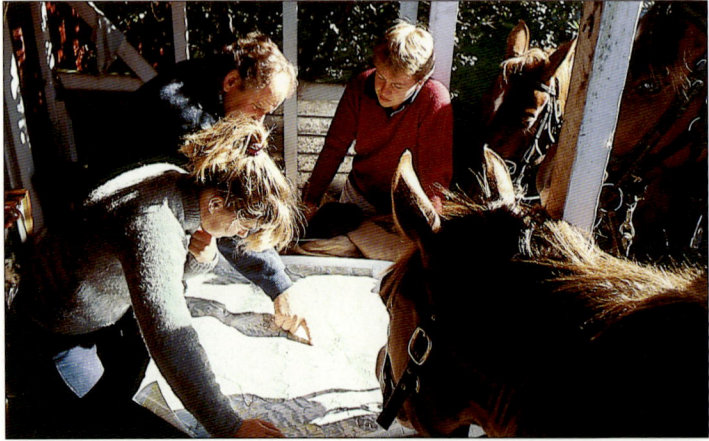

Monty map reading as John Shearer points out the route!

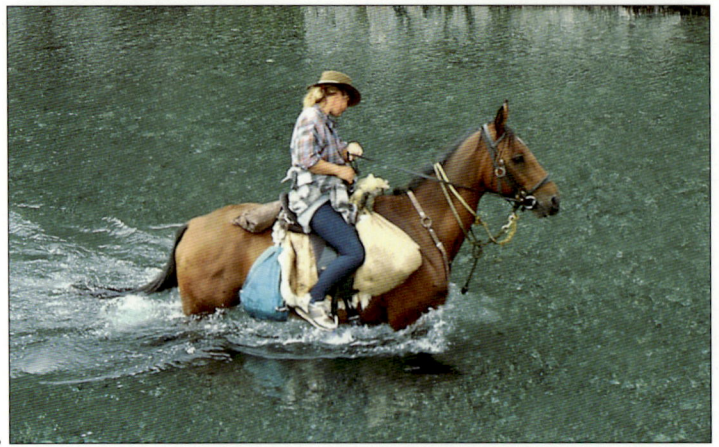

Ali riding Nelson upsteam

New Zealand Geographic Magazine had given us the task of retracing the steps of the first Europeans across the Southern Alps to the West Coast. Over a hundred years ago Leonard Harper and his Maori guides had found the traverse so hazardous they had had to leave their horses on the eastern slope of the Alps and had arrived on the West Coast in rafts. There they discovered gold, which led to an unprecedented gold rush of 4,000 fortune-seekers struggling across the Southern Alps to stake their claim in the West Coast gold fields. Their horses were bogged down, men became half starved, and many drowned in the Taramakau, nicknamed Digger's Grave.

We had invited Wayne, a friend, to join us. I had flippantly suggested in Auckland that he might like a quick jaunt across the Alps. To my surprise he accepted the offer but we were to discover it was more like an epic journey rather than a jaunt! He was not nearly as fit as Ali and I after travelling over 1500 miles and he had no experience with horses.

Three days into our trek from Hanmer Springs towards the Southern Alps, we saddled up before dawn and forged ahead up a valley flanked by snow topped mountains. Ali, leading the way, was riding Honey over some wet logs acting as a bridge when Honey's hooves slipped and Ali and Honey disappeared into a deep ditch. I dashed to the edge, my heart pounding as Honey frantically thrashed around on top of Ali as she tried to regain her footing.

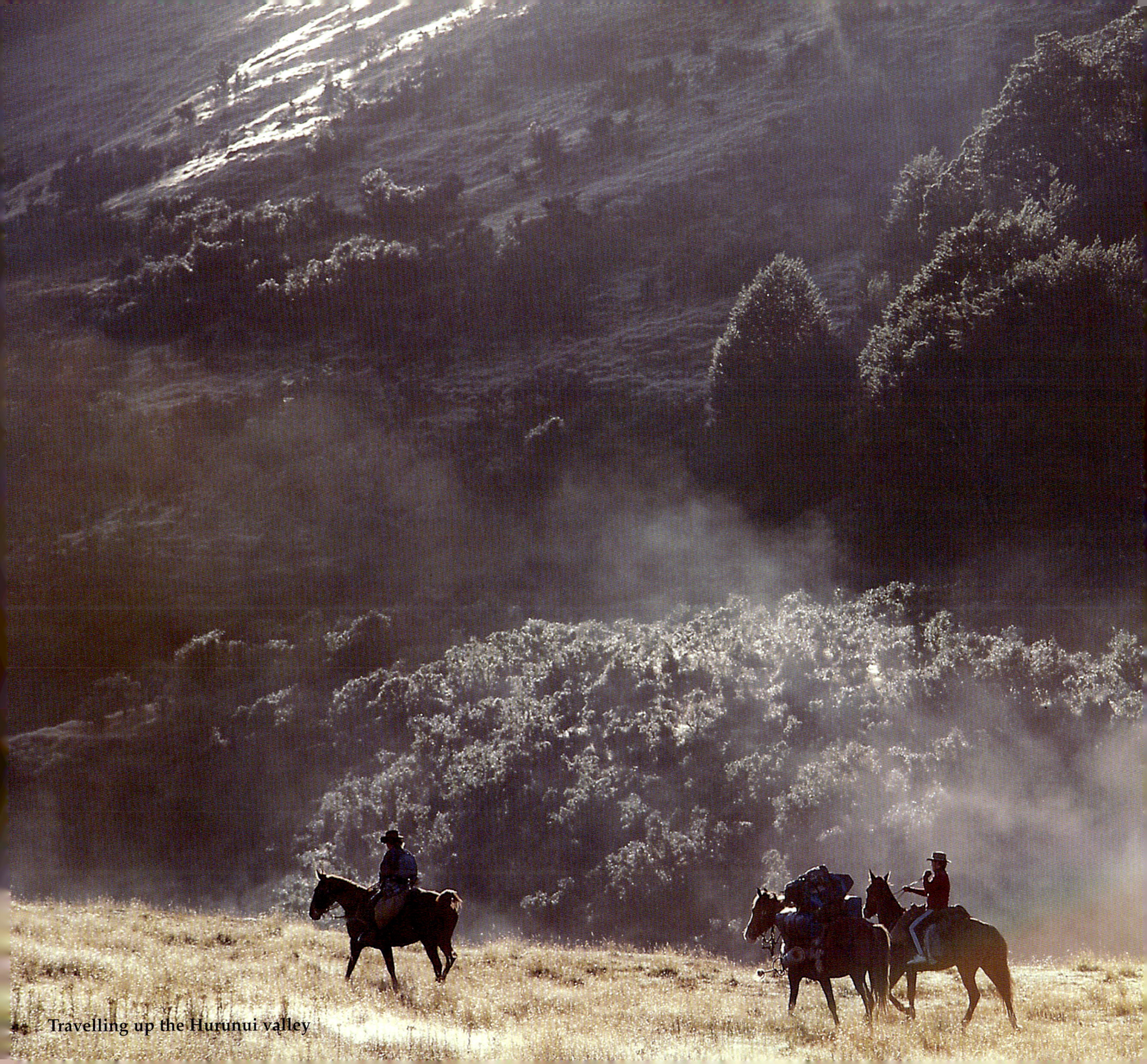
Travelling up the Hurunui valley

30
Cliff Edge

Call me and I'll answer, be at your side in bad times; I'll rescue you, Psalm 91:15 TM

Miraculously, first Honey emerged then Ali scrambled out, scratched, shaken but unhurt. Tremendously relieved, we thanked God and soothed Honey who was trembling with shock. After wringing out Ali's clothes we continued up the valley, carefully picking our route through dangerous swamp land where our horses sank up to their stomachs, plunging and splashing mud in all directions.

"Be sure to stay up close to the tree-line," John Shearer had warned us, "More than a hundred horses have been lost in those swamps." This route had been described in the gold rush days as *a half-liquid marsh strewn with the skeletons of pack horses, their bones picked clean by bush rats.*

We pressed on up the Hurunui river, with the occasional deviation through the bush and endless crossing and re-crossing of the river. The valley grew progressively narrower until it was confined to riverbed boulders and rushing water. When it became impossible to travel in the river we forged our path through the moss-hung forest, manoeuvring the horses over rotting logs and squeezing between trees. At one place a landslide had obliterated all semblance of a track and only a narrow ledge of scree remained, which plummeted 30 feet to the river below. A large rock projecting on to the scree made the prospect of crossing the ledge even more daunting, but there was no alternative. Unloading the packs off Monty we slid them across the gap, then praying, we dashed across leading our horses.

We camped on the east side of the pass and endeavoured to heat some soup but the firewood was so damp it produced only a mass of smoke. We had estimated the whole crossing to take five days but we hadn't even got to the summit and already we had finished Moira's delicious and substantial oat biscuits. The remainder of our boring food supply was dwindling so we had to put ourselves on rations, although exhausted by ploughing through such rough terrain, which continually ripped off our horses' shoes. By this stage of our ride we had learned to shoe the horses ourselves, when necessary but it was a laborious task which took hours using a donated garage rasp and lightweight hammer. The horses became understandably impatient, wrenching their hooves out of our grasp and leaning hard on us.

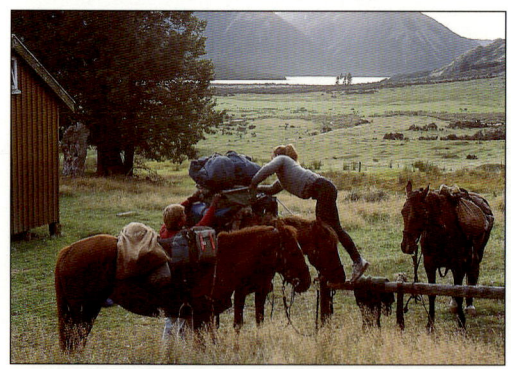
Morning pack-up near Lake Sumner

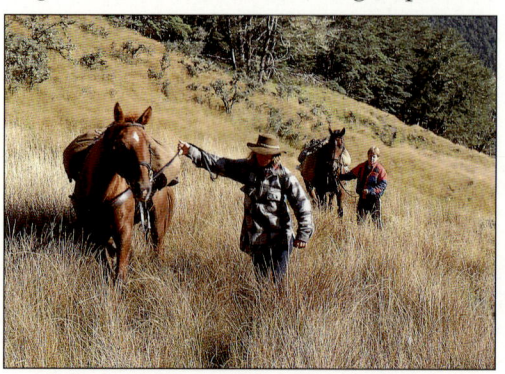
Picking our way through the bog

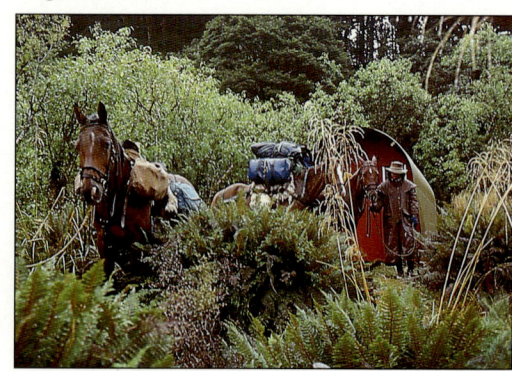
The drizzle increased to a downpour

That night I dreamt of escaped horses and slippery river boulders. Prophetic perhaps, for in the morning we discovered Monty had snapped his tethering rope and had disappeared with Nelson, leaving Honey still tied up and distraught at being abandoned. Recalling earlier warnings of deer stalkers in the area, we hurriedly set out to track them, following hoofprints that led back the way we had come. Wading through thigh-deep water, we criss-crossed the Hurunui before finally sighting them. By the time we had returned to camp with the horses the rain had increased to a downpour. From then on, it was a fight scrambling up a slippery, steep gradient to the pass over the rocky headwaters of the Hurunui. Monty fell twice, finding it difficult with the weight of his packs to regain his footing. On the narrow ledge he fell yet again and lay pivoting on his stomach with his hind legs hanging over a precipitous drop.

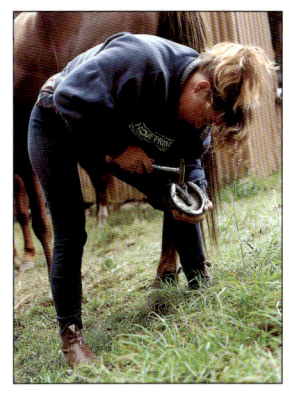

Ali shoeing Monty

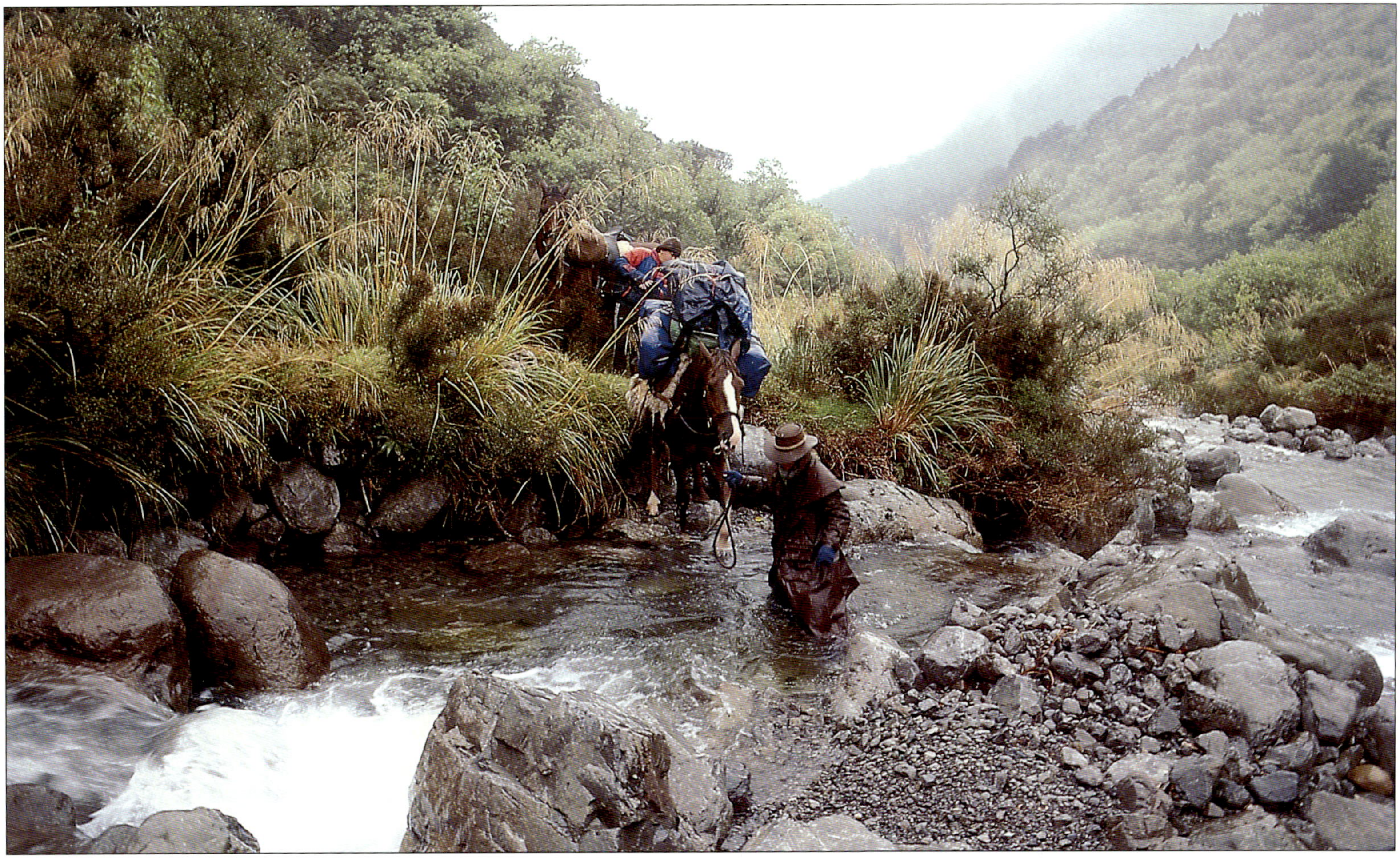

Ali leading Monty across the head waters of the Hurunui

31
DIGGER'S GRAVE

When you pass through the waters, I will be with you; and through the rivers, they shall not overflow you.
Isaiah 43:2 NKJ

I yelled at Monty as he lay on the ledge suspended over the cliff and with a supreme effort and extraordinary strength, he managed to hook his front hooves into the ledge and heave himself back onto the track. Tears, from the aftershock and relief blurred my vision, as we stroked Monty and thanked God for saving him from certain death.

In continual driving rain we scrambled to the crest of the divide, which was shrouded in cloud. Before us lay the turbulent Taramakau river valley, known in the 1860s as Digger's Grave because its raging waters had claimed so many lives. The western descent proved much steeper than the ascent. We followed a rough track dropping 400 metres in the first two miles, through sub-alpine vegetation and beech forest. Then we were swallowed into the dark bush. In many places the track had been washed away, leaving steep drops ringed by tangled roots. Down these we had to coax and manoeuvre our horses. One moment they would refuse to move; the next, following so closely behind us, they trod on our heels or knocked us over as they slid uncontrollably in the mud. Wayne probably suffered the most as he was unfamiliar with horses. Monty, wearing his cumbersome pack, got himself into almost inextricable positions, wedged between and under tree trunks. Often fallen trees blocked our path and when we couldn't squeeze past or move them, we were forced to fight our way through the dense dripping undergrowth.

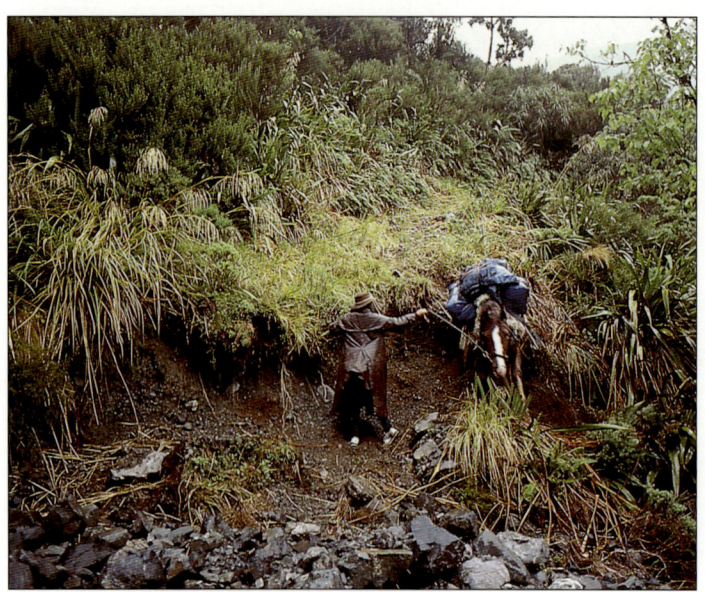

Ali guiding Monty down a steep drop

As we continually criss-crossed the river, the water rose up to our waists and was still rising when we found a hut on the bank. Exhausted and deciding it was too dangerous to go on we took advantage of some shelter. We were so sorry for our horses who had cuts on their swollen legs and were foot sore from having their shoes ripped off in the riverbed. Ours were also ripped and both my bruised feet protruded out of the gaping holes at the sides, making it very difficult to walk.

Eventually we managed to light a fire with damp wood, we draped our wet clothes over the rafters and around the smoking fire which stung our eyes, making them water. Cold and hungry we curled up in our wet sleeping bags.

The following morning the raging river was up another foot. Streams gushed in all directions, dragging with them logs and scrub. Physically exhausted, I stared at what we had to cross; a hypnotising, furious mass of black water, which drummed threateningly in my ears.

32
THE OTIRA

*Be strong and very courageous. Do not be terrified; do not be discouraged,
for the Lord your God will be with you wherever you go.* Joshua 1:9 NIV

It was too dangerous to go on, so we shared our last cup of soup, feeling too weak to grovel for berries in the dripping bush, following instructions from *How to survive in the Mountains, in the Bush and on the Coast*! A book Ali had carried all the way from Cape Reinga. We lost the weight gained through people's hospitality in the North Island and I feebly joked, "Hey Ali, if we'd stuck to our goal of living off the land, we'd have certainly starved to death long ago!"

Stranded by the roaring, swollen river with the rain hammering on the tin roof we prayed the raging storm would stop. After several hours, I dragged myself out to re-shoe Monty but he was so footsore he repeatedly snatched his foot from my grasp. This struggle sapped the last of my energy and suddenly a rusty nail ripped into my hand. I knew this was really serious, and with blood oozing from the gash I abandoned the job. Back in the hut with my whole arm throbbing, I couldn't remember when I had last had a tetanus injection. With no way of getting to a hospital my only option was to rely on God's healing. At dawn the following morning, Ali shouted, "Trace, the rain has stopped! We've got to get out of here now!" Scrambling together our sodden belongings, I realised my arm was miraculously healed.

Threatening black clouds filled us with a desperate urgency to escape the valley, but the daunting prospect of finding a way to cross the raging torrent needed all our courage. I waded in leading Honey, but as I left the river bank the current was too strong and I could hardly stand. Honey continued to the other side while I had to back track. Next, I rode Nelson across and discovered that horses had better balance. With the water over our stirrups, we rode with our feet loose so that if they stumbled, we wouldn't be trapped. Drowning was the most common cause of death in New Zealand a hundred years ago.

The only way to proceed, as the surrounding bush was impenetrable, was to repeatedly cross and re-cross the Taramakau river. We felt acutely responsible for our miserable, footsore horses. The usually jovial Monty hung his head and limped badly. We ripped up one empty feed sack and tied it around his hooves but it got sodden and continually slipped as we forded the Taramakau through the day and into the night, guided only by the feeble beam of a pocket torch. When the batteries died we followed vague impressions of light and dark on the riverbank. Occasionally the moon broke through, and at one point we found ourselves on swampy ground surrounded by ghost-like tree stumps. The ground quivering beneath us, we quickly stumbled back to the riverbank.

Midnight arrived and so did the last tributary to cross, The Otira. With another impending flash flood we were desperate to escape the valley. Mounted on Nelson, our intrepid leader, and praying continuously, I nervously guided him into the dark waters to find a crossing. All I could see and feel were the white caps of water and the strong current flowing between his legs. Suddenly he stopped and when I urged him forwards he refused and swivelling around, took me back to the bank. Clearly the crossing was too dangerous so we collapsed on to the bank for the remainder of the night, praying that we wouldn't be trapped by another storm.

33
EASTER DAY!

You broaden the path beneath me, so that my ankles do not turn. Psalm 18:36 NIV

On Easter Day we awoke to shafts of sunshine squeezing through the clouds and warming our damp bodies. We were thankful that it hadn't rained again in the night as we forded the wide Otira river in stages. We headed through some trees in what we guessed to be the direction of human habitation, the first we would have seen for eight days!

Bedraggled and footsore, all of us very much lighter in weight than the previous week, we emerged from the bush and approached a small wooden house.

"Would you have a paddock we could put our horses in?" Ali asked, as we introduced ourselves to a young man called Scott and his friend, Aran, who peered over his shoulder on the doorstep.

"We've been stuck on the pass and neither we nor our horses have eaten for several days." I added.

"Ar, my uncle Ernie is down at Kumara pub but I'm sure it'll be fine to use the deer paddock," he stuttered, with a bemused look on his face. We unsaddled the horses and they all had a thorough roll before putting their heads down for some serious eating! We did likewise with a tomato sandwich, which had never tasted so good!

That afternoon Wayne caught a lift with Scott and Aran to Christchurch, where he caught a plane back to Auckland. He bid us farewell, remarking that the trip had strengthened his faith, and with a laugh added,

"But girls, don't ever ask me to come on holiday with you again!"

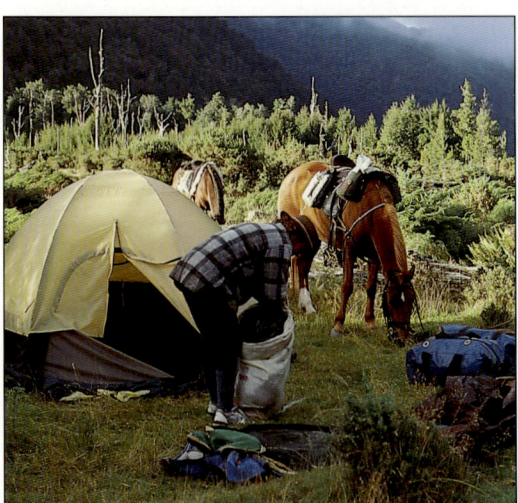

Ali packing up on the banks of the Otira river

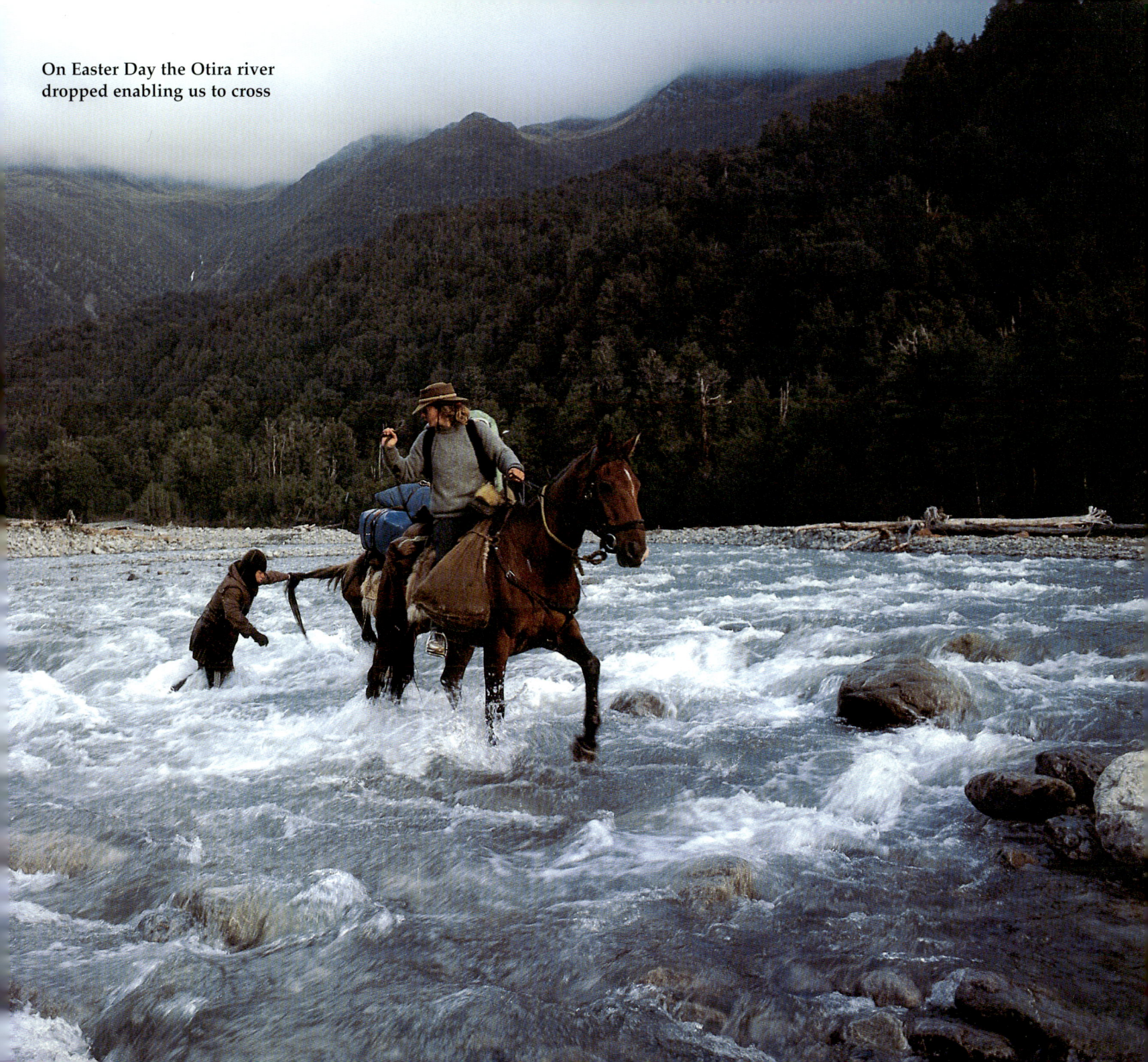

On Easter Day the Otira river dropped enabling us to cross

34
CHRISTCHURCH

If God is for us, who can ever be against us? Romans 8:31 NLT

Ernie stayed celebrating down at the Kumara pub that night, oblivious to the strangers staying in his house. The storm which had been threatening for several days broke and the brewing sky exploded. Rain lashed against the bowing windows and the ferocious wind shook and rattled the little wooden house and once more flooded the Taramakau river valley.

It was so comforting inside! In true West Coast style Ernie, who returned after a couple of nights, invited us to stay as long as we liked.

"You couldn't have come to a nicer bloke's door!" one man said. However, once the horses had recovered and been professionally shod, we were compelled to press on to Christchurch to follow up on further visa extensions.

"We're outlaws on horseback, now our visas have expired!" I joked at the truth as our horses' hooves echoed along the Arthur's Pass road, which had superseded Harper's, leading us back across the Southern Alps.

"God is on our side," Ali declared confidently, " And the whole country knows about our expedition!"

Just on the eastern slope of the Alps we left our horses on a station to save them the long 150 mile deviation on hard roads. Hitch-hiking into the beautiful garden city of Christchurch, we fund raised with a borrowed race horse called Mr Richmond, who had won ten races before retiring.

Parliament grudgingly consented, allowing up to three more months on our visas. After a week in the city we sorely missed our horses and were keen to get back into the wide open spaces.

We hitch-hiked out of Christchurch with a 25 kilogramme sack of grain. Our horses looked pleased to see us, as they stretched their necks over a wire fence, or was it the sack of grain we grasped between us as we struggled up the stony track!

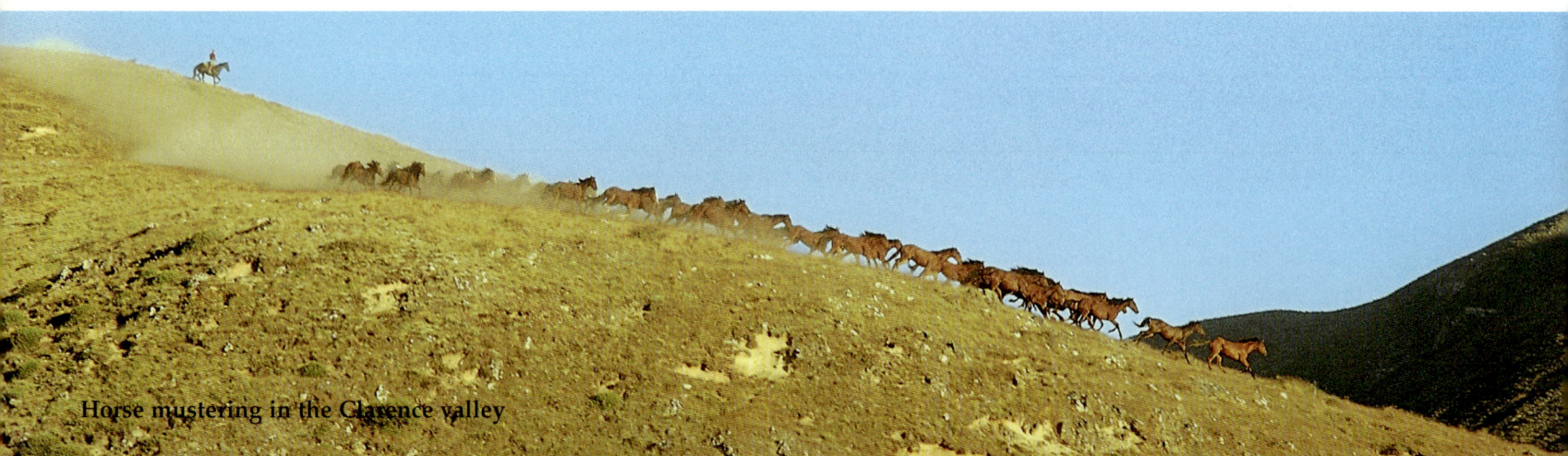
Horse mustering in the Clarence valley

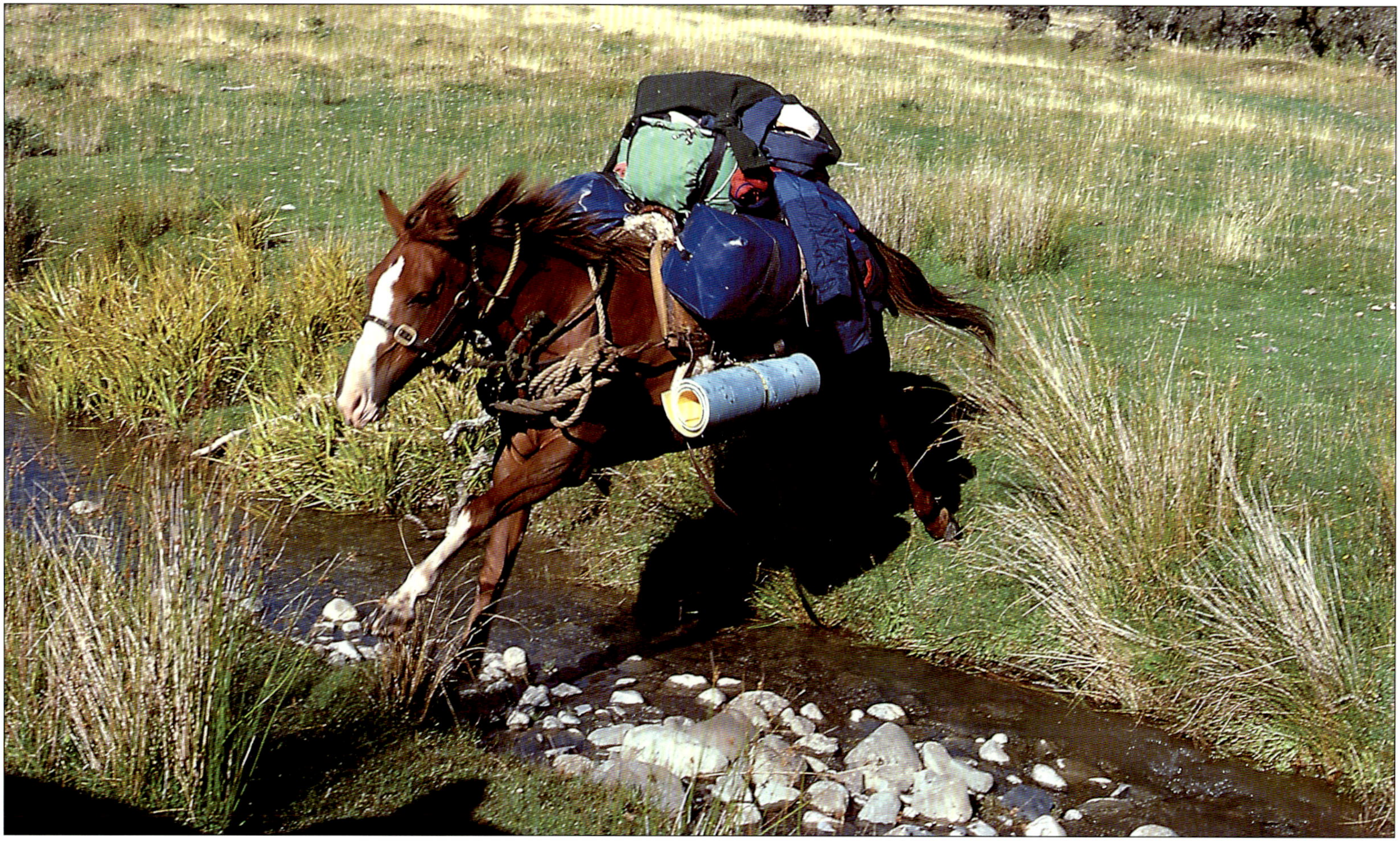

Monty taking a short cut!

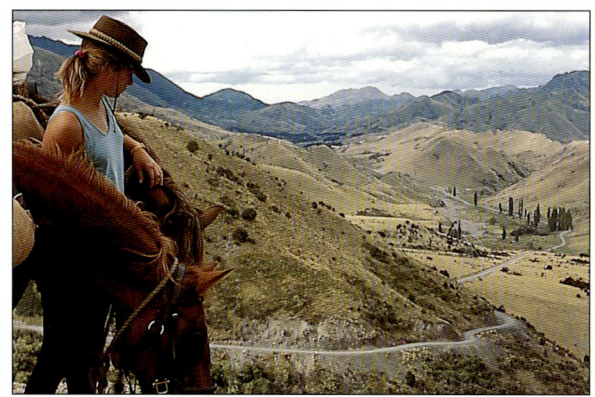
Ali with Honey and Nelson

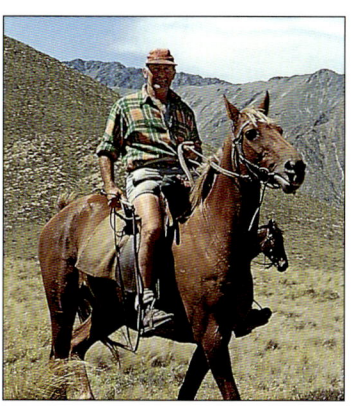
Earl Lunn horse mustering

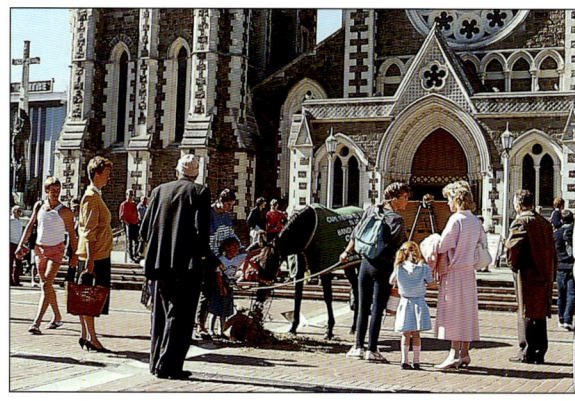
Fund raising in Christchurch

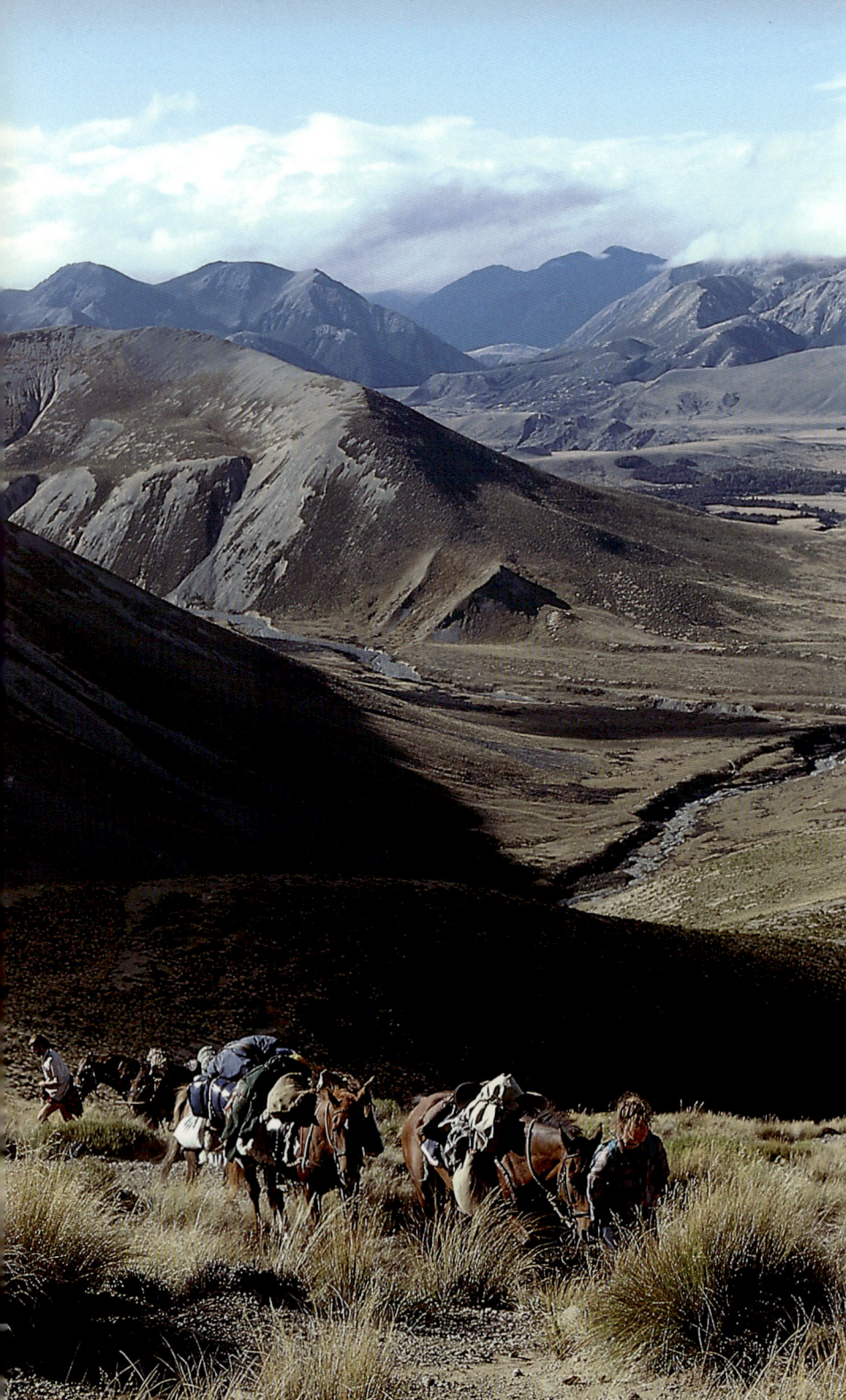

35
COLERIDGE SADDLE

*Whenever trouble comes your way,
let it be an opportunity for joy.* James 1:2 NLT

After city life it was great to be back in the saddle again, riding through the wide open spaces of the High Country. A young German man, who worked on the station where we had left our horses, offered to be our guide. We had planned for some easy riding after the Harpers Pass episode but instead of riding the longer way by road, we accepted his offer to guide us over the Coleridge Saddle. We soon regretted this, when we discovered he had never been this way before! At midnight we found ourselves stuck on a mountain pass surrounded by matagouri, a very spiky bush used by the Maoris in the past for tattooing.

"I'm staying here!" our guide suddenly announced, interrupting his constant complaining about being spiked by the matagouri, and proceeded to roll out his sleeping bag on the dark steep mountain slope, with nothing for his horse to eat.
"But we need to find food for our horses!" Ali said urgently, "they haven't eaten all day.'
"I'm staying," he stated. "You go on if you want."
"Okay, goodbye then!" We agreed that the welfare of our horses was of the utmost importance, as we pressed on and out of the matagouri.
'Wow! It's so peaceful now!" Ali sighed as the moon peaked out of the clouds and our horses cast elongated shadows across the rough ground.
"I agree!" I laughed, adding, "After Harper Pass, nothing can be as bad!"

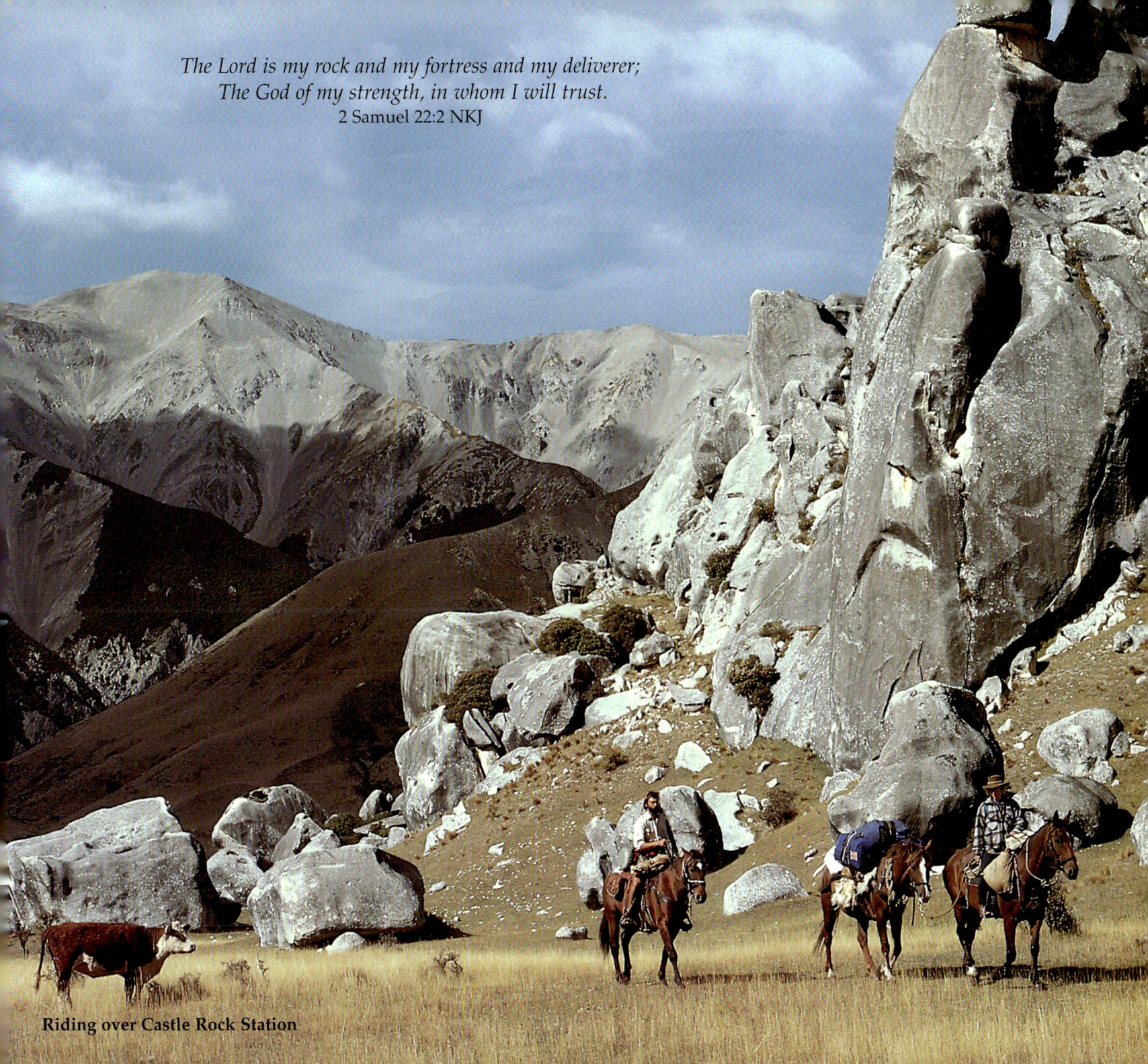

*The Lord is my rock and my fortress and my deliverer;
The God of my strength, in whom I will trust.*
2 Samuel 22:2 NKJ

Riding over Castle Rock Station

36
THE HIGH COUNTRY

It is impossible that no offenses should come. Luke 17:1 NKJ

We continued through the majestic and mountainous High Country, cautiously fording wide intertwining rivers, which often concealed dangerous underlying quicksand.

It was early April and the morning landscape often glistened with frost as we set off, wrapped up in gloves, scarves and hats. By mid-morning, we had gradually peeled them off and rode on in our shorts.

We also rode though a snow blizzard, wearing all the clothes we possessed, our scarves wrapped up to our eyes, our hats pulled down over our foreheads, seeing only a few feet ahead of us through the whirling snow. We were greatly relieved to find a station later that day where our horses were given food and shelter, while we thawed out in a shepherd's hut. Steam rose from our damp clothes draped around the hot fire, toasting our hands and faces and melting my shoes, (the pair I had recently bought for $2 in a second-hand shop in Christchurch, to replace those which had disintegrated over Harper's!). We had to drag ourselves away from the cosy fireplace to the bunk beds where we slept in our clothes, woolly hats and gloves as the blizzard continued to rattle the hut throughout the night. At dawn, the thin layer of snow carpeting the countryside soon vanished under the warm sun.

It was in the stunning High Country, that our route was blocked by one land-owner, who refused us permission to cross his land,

"You're girls and will probably get lost!" His words stung.

"We might only be girls but we've just ridden over 1,500 miles and we need to come through your place to continue our route southward." I retorted and then reasoned, trying to persuade him to change his mind, but he refused. I was irritated and upset, as his refusal blocked our route through some spectacular mountain scenery which I had been looking forward to photographing. I knew taking the smouldering offence with me would spoil whatever lay ahead, so I adjusted my attitude and decided to forgive and bless him instead. It became more sincere with **practice!**

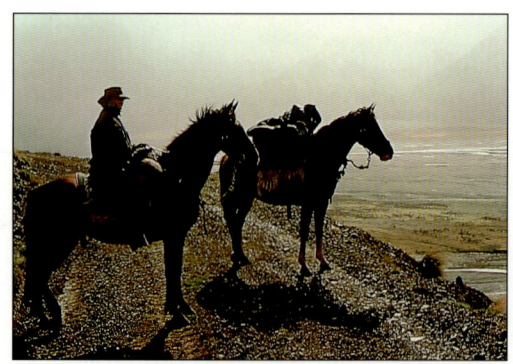
Sunshine interrupts a snowstorm

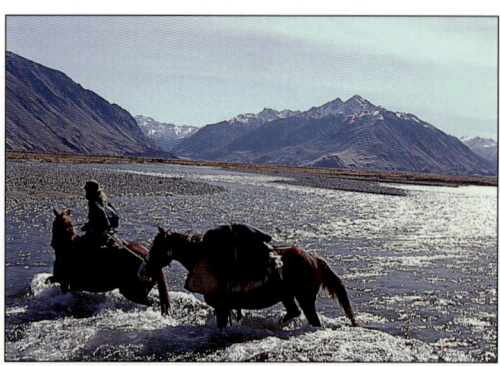
Fording the Rakaia River

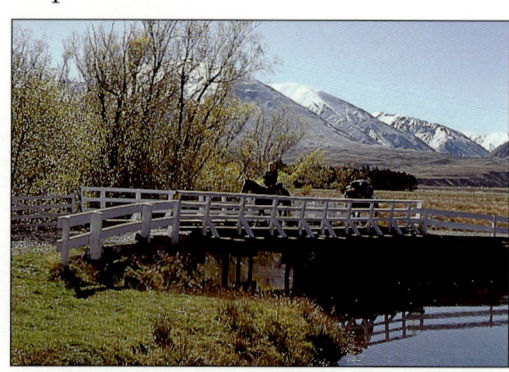
Crossing over near Lake Heron

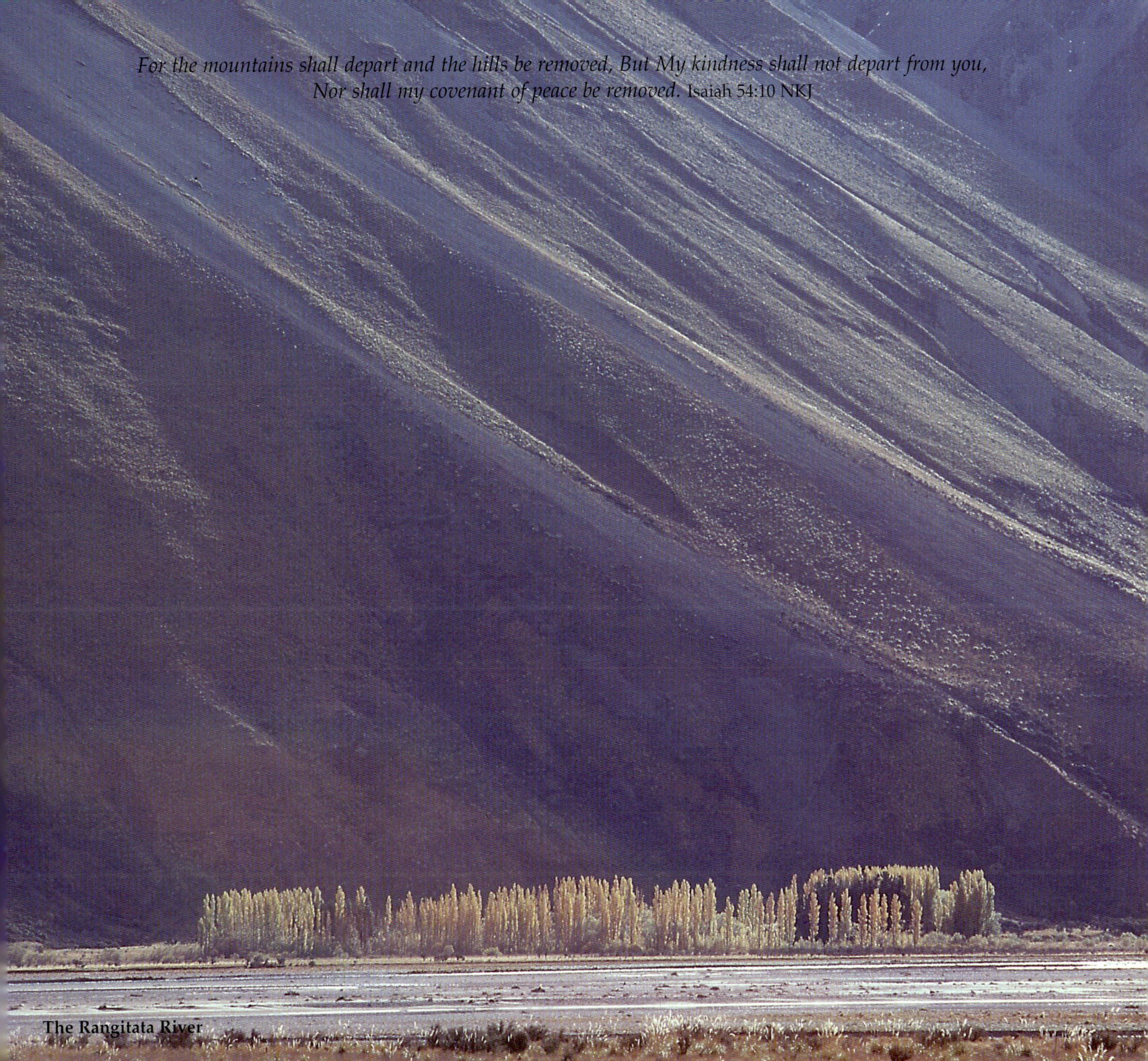

For the mountains shall depart and the hills be removed, But My kindness shall not depart from you, Nor shall my covenant of peace be removed. Isaiah 54:10 NKJ

The Rangitata River

37

THE RANGITATA

Then will you delight yourself in the Lord, and I will make you to ride on the high places of the earth. Isaiah 58:14 Amp

We had no option but to ride eastwards, back towards the drought stricken area which we so much wanted to avoid. We followed the banks of the Rangitata river and stayed at Ben Mcleod Station, where the owners Donald and Sue Aubrey called ahead for permission for us to ride across Rata Peak station.

The temperature climbed with us upwards along a steep winding track. Behind us the tall poplar trees appeared as small golden dots beside the Rangitata river, which flowed as glistening interwoven strands from the base of the snow-capped mountains.

Descending eastwards we once again entered the drought which had dehydrated the whole of the East Coast. We rode through a gate with a warning of 1080 poison and had to keep Monty on the lead as scattered over the hillside were poisoned carrots. Monty was disgruntled he wasn't allowed to eat the only food available! As our horses' hooves thudded on the hard ground creating dust clouds, we were concerned and asked God somehow to supply food for our horses in this desert-like place.

The temperature plummeted with the sun and to keep warm, we trotted on through the gloom and into a blanket of cold mist, hanging over the barren plain.

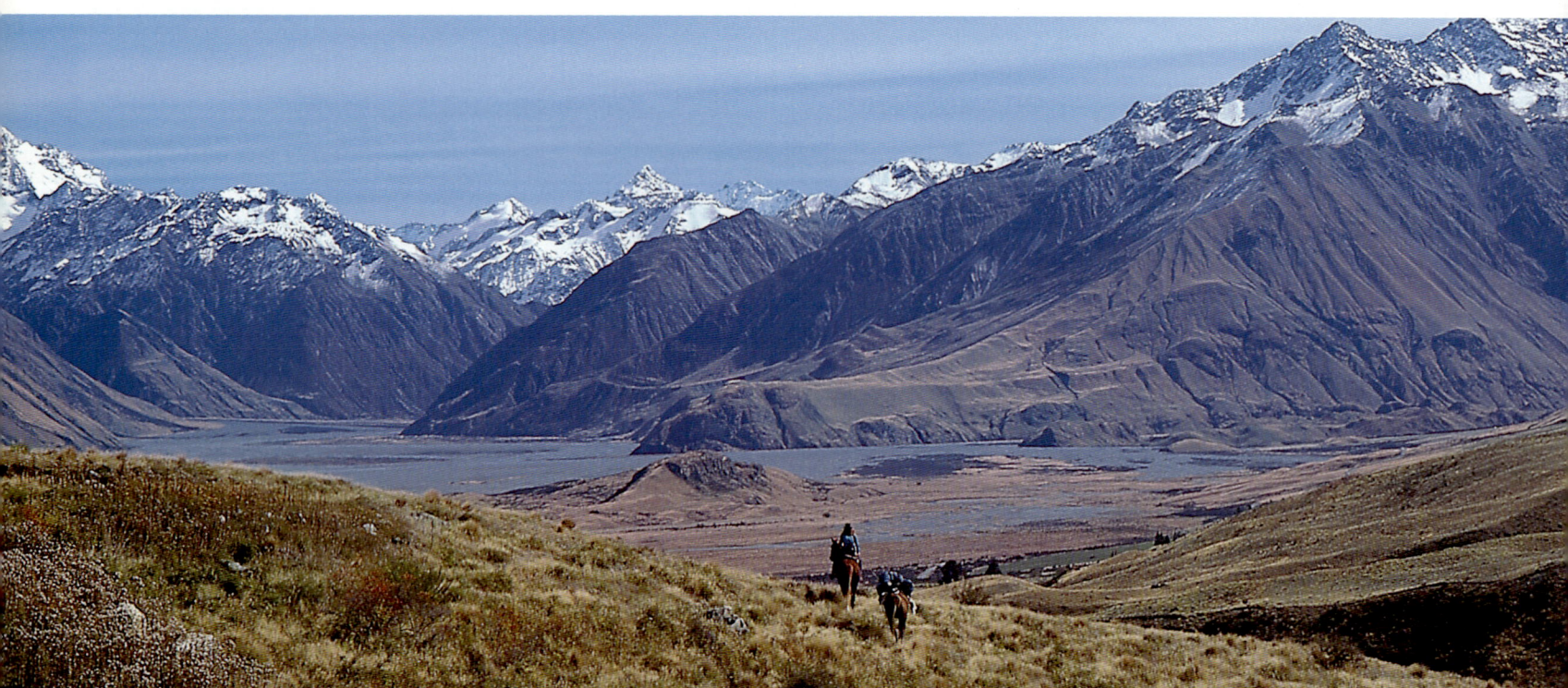

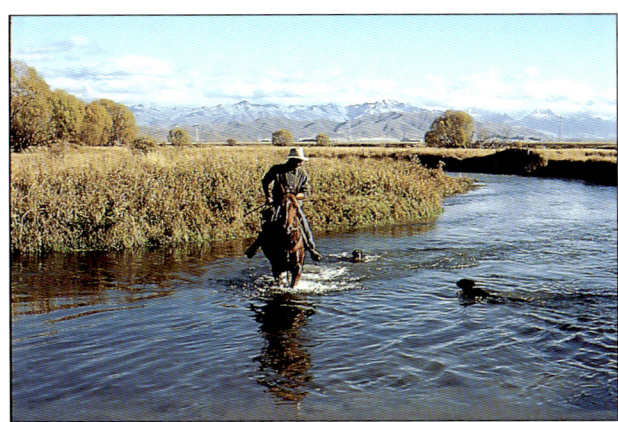 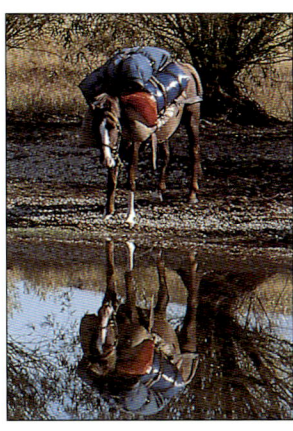 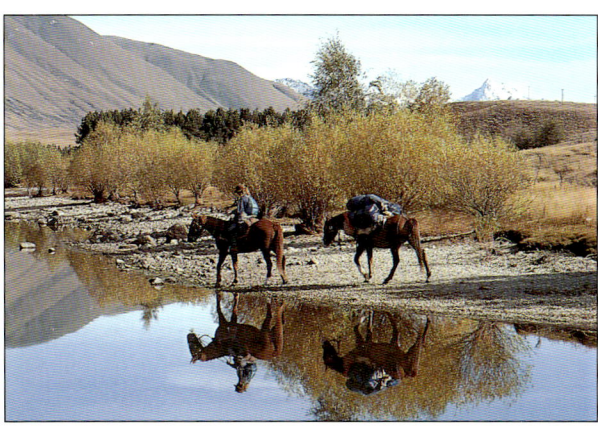

Ferg and his dogs from Grays Hill Station
Below: Looking back up the Rangitata river basin

"What a handsome horse!" Monty sees his reflection!

Lake Clearwater with Mount Cook in the distance

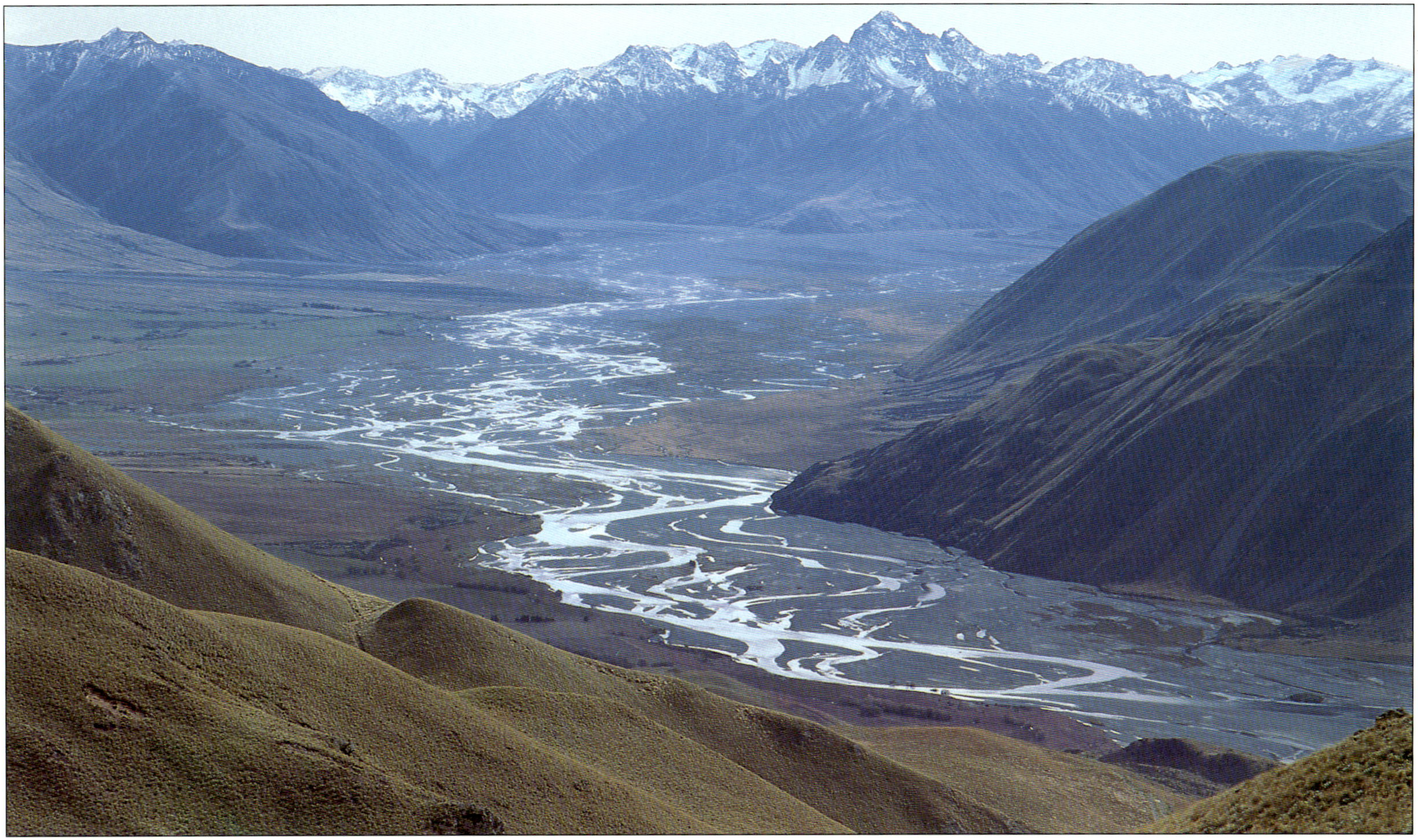

38
CLAYTON STATION

Your faithfulness reaches to the skies. Psalm 57:10 NIV

Trotting on through the twilight across the plain to seemingly nowhere a four-wheel drive vehicle passed us, leaving us shrouded in dust. The cloud had just settled when it did a u-turn up the road and I thought, "Oh no, here comes another dust bath!'
   This time it slowed down when passing us and the driver leant out of his window.
   'Where are you girls going ?'
   "Bluff." Ali replied.
   "'Well, you won't get there tonight!" introducing himself as Andrew Orbell he added,
   "Why not come home with me!"
   So we followed his dust trail for about a mile and then turned into a complex of houses and barns. As we wound between dusty yards of hungry looking animals, which either raced up to us in curiosity or away in fright, I doubted whether there would be any food for the horses.
   "Well, at least our horses won't escape tonight!" I remarked to Ali.
   Suddenly, rounding a bend in the fence, our ears pricked as Andrew stopped outside the main homestead next to an enclosed paddock of lush grass six inches high!
   "Girls, is this all right for your horses?"
Both we and our horses were delighted at such an extravagant answer to our prayer as they enjoyed a good roll before indulging in some serious eating! Then Andrew and his wife Ruth invited us in to eat and we slept in a comfortable room, a luxurious contrast to our usual accommodation of stark shearer's quarters or our tiny tent!

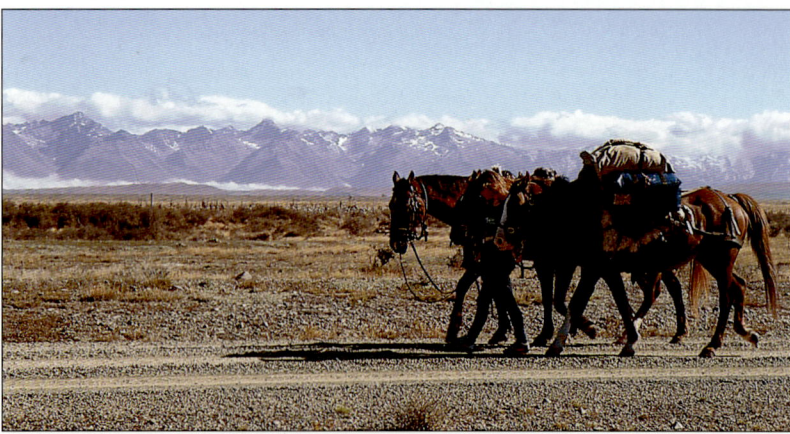

84 Ali leading Nelson, Honey and Monty across the Mackenzie plains

The Lindis Pass

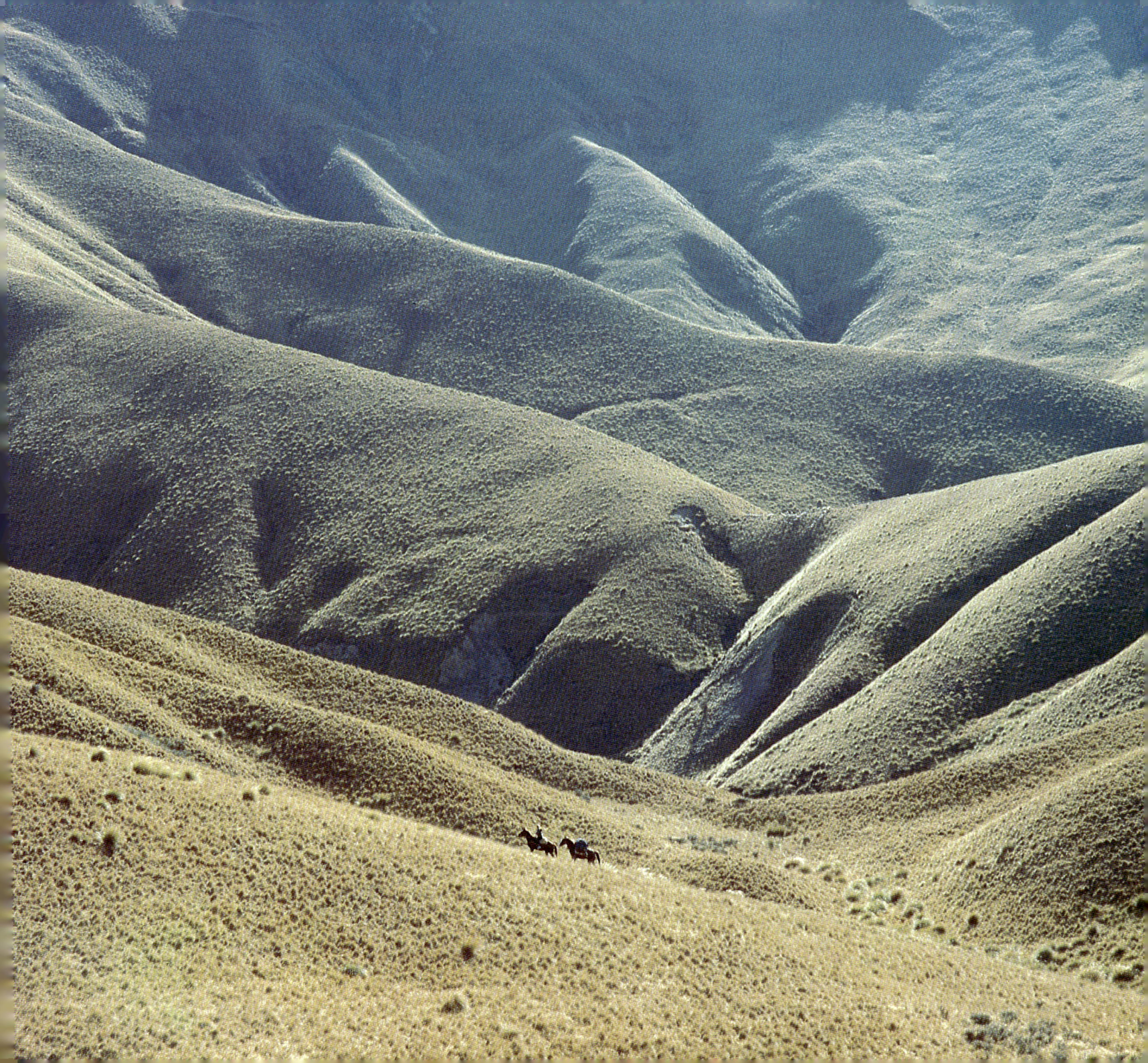

39
THE MACKENZIE COUNTRY

*You will show me the path of life;
In Your presence is fullness of joy;
At Your right hand are pleasures
forevermore.* Psalm 16:11NKJ

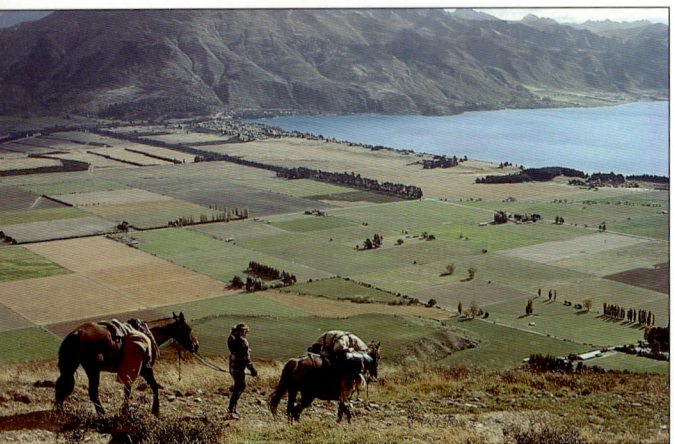
Ferg and his horses at Grays Hill Station

Descending to Lake Hawea

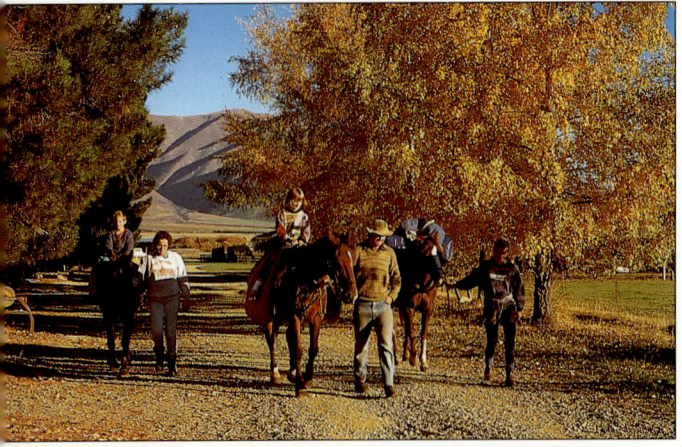
The Twoddle family seeing us off from Clifton Downs

The MacKenzie country got its name from an infamous sheep rustler and his dog, who rustled thousands of sheep. It is a vast plain strewn with stones and rabbit holes, which made travelling any faster than a walk very hazardous. Nelson put his foot down one hole and as he fell I was catapulted off over his head. We both scrambled to our feet unhurt, whereas Monty, putting his hoof down another hole, twisted his hind leg more seriously. We stopped at Grays Hill Station while waiting for him to recover and helped out mustering cattle and shearing sheep.

After several days rest, Monty had recovered and we continued on, across the Lindis Pass, over an ocean of swaying brown tussock grass shimmering in the sun and wind. Once on the other side we crossed Black Forest Station and descended onto the chequered plain of Lake Hawea. Then, south to the beautiful blue Lake Wanaka, trimmed with contrasting golden poplar trees and surrounded by stark rugged mountains.

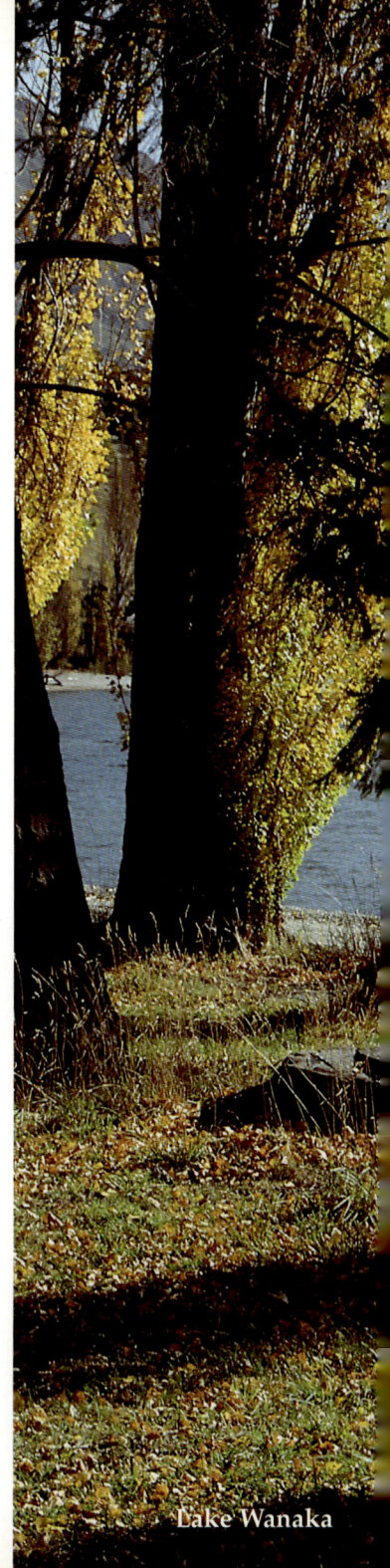
Lake Wanaka

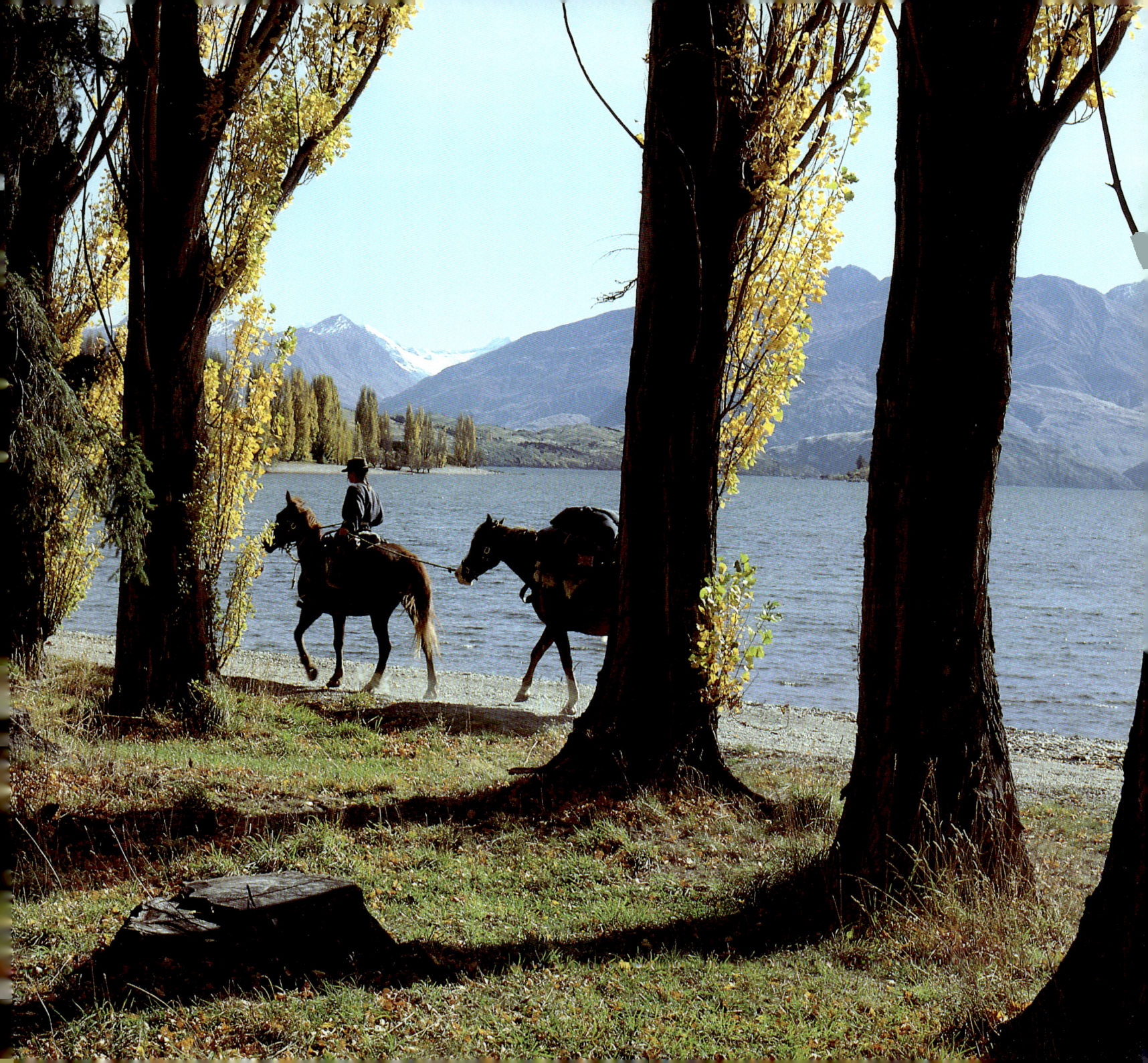

40
QUEENSTOWN

God has made everything beautiful in its time. Ecclesiastes 3:11 NIV

On route to Queenstown we followed the Arrow river, which was edged with a colourful array of autumn golds, reds and browns. We rode into Arrowtown, our horses' hooves echoing up a street lined with colourful storefronts preserved as a replica of the gold mining days. We felt like cowboys, boots resounding on the wooden board walk, as we entered through swinging saloon doors.

That night we fed hay to our horses in Lindsey and Elizabeth Keys' garden and the next day rode on to Queenstown, where we fund raised, amidst a mass of tourists. Tony McQuilkin, the owner of the Earnslaw, a steamer taking excursion trips round Lake Wakatipu, offered to take our horses across to the other side to save us a long ride round. But the horses weren't so sure and refused to board!

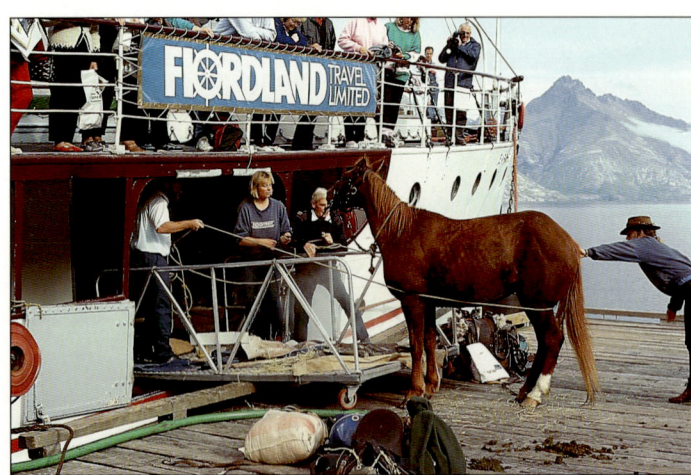

Honey refusing to board the Earnslaw at Queenstown

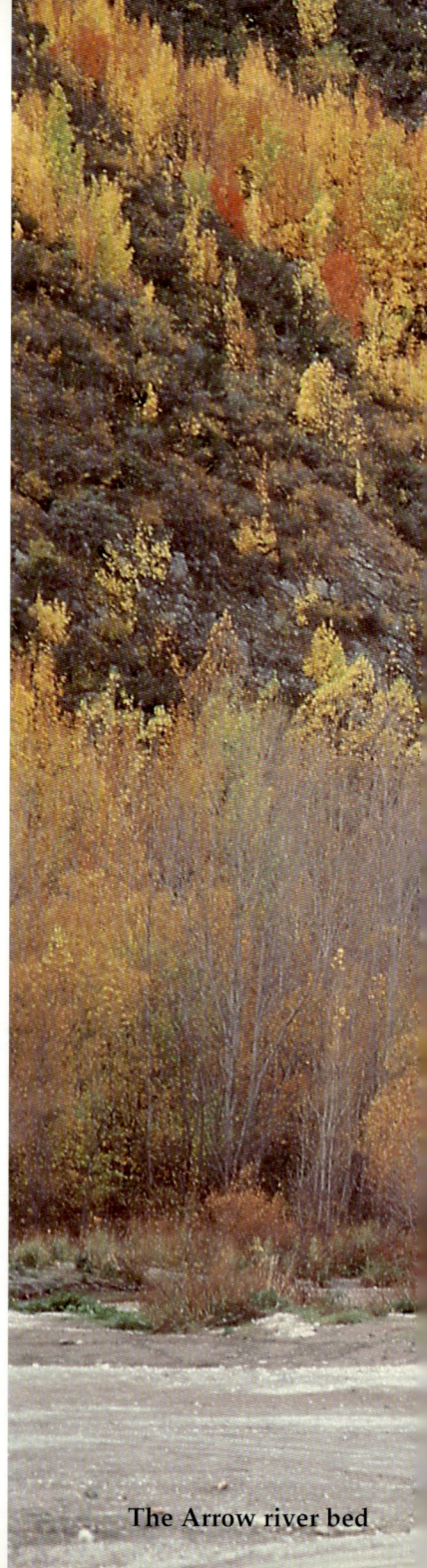

The Arrow river bed

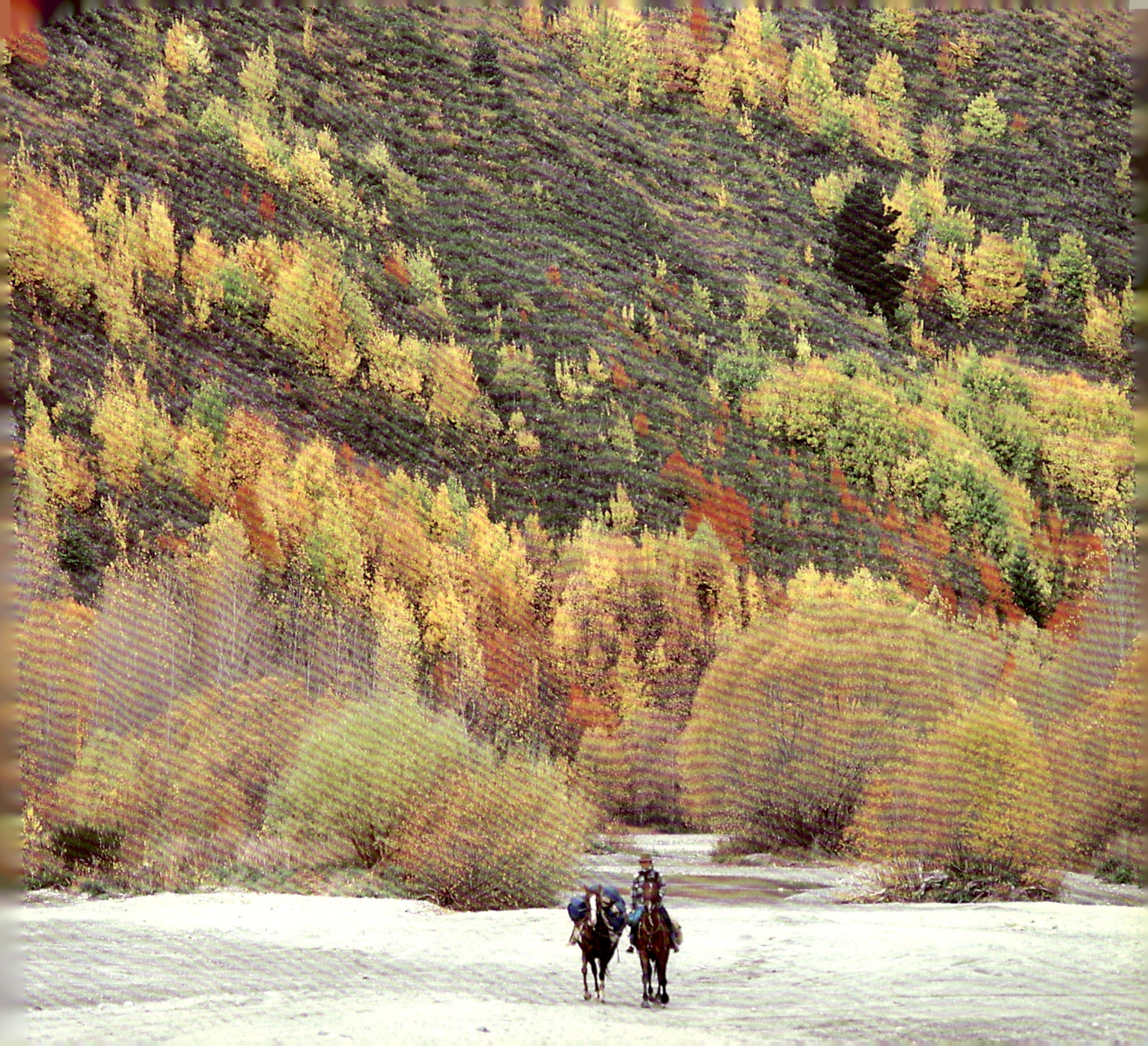

41
MONTY'S FALL

The Lord protects them from harm - not one of their bones will be broken! Psalm 34:20 NLT

As we headed south through the cold rain we felt the chill of winter upon us. We had been riding for six months from November, New Zealand's springtime, through to May, when the leaves had fallen from the trees. Suddenly, our nomadic life, taking each day as it came, was drawing to an end. Although the expedition had often been a test of endurance, continually on the move, sometimes physically exhausted, while travelling into the night and sleeping rough, we felt heavy hearted to be nearing the end of our 2,000 mile ride.

But I almost didn't make it!

Cantering along the roadside verge, out of Invercargill after our last day fund raising, Monty stumbled crossing some gravel and fell on top of me and the camera round my neck. His heavy weight squashed all the breath out of my body and pinned me to the ground.

Ali rolled Monty carefully off me, so that he wouldn't roll over my head. I felt numbed, like a squashed cartoon character, Steam rollered, flattened by a door falling off its hinges, with an Olympus camera insignia impressed on my chest!

Miraculously, although stunned and gasping for breath, I sat on the gravel with no broken bones. Meanwhile Monty, with only a grazed nose stood beside me and sniffed at me apologetically! Ali helped me back on my feet and gave me a leg up back onto Nelson who was our favourite to ride as he had a more comfortable pace. Continuing at a walk we eventually reached our destination for the night. But I couldn't move, my body had stiffened up and I was stuck in my saddle, set like a statue on my horse!

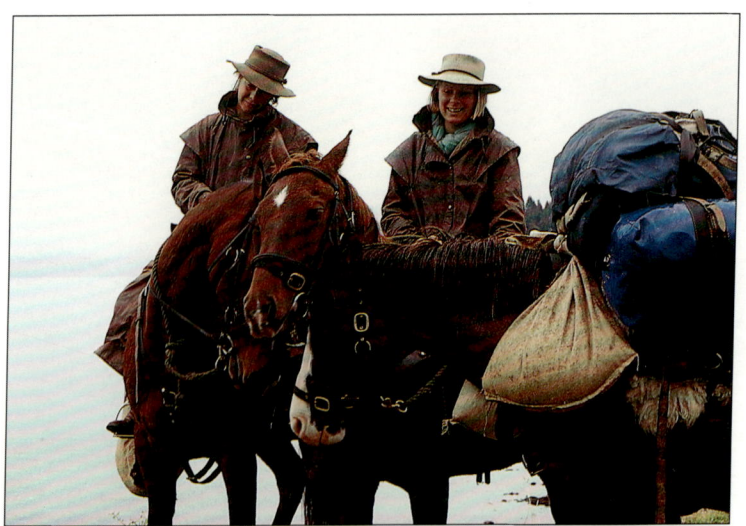
Ali on Nelson, Tracey on Honey and Monty carrying the pack

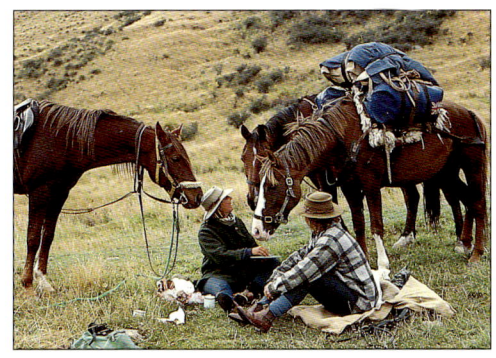
Picnic time with the horses!

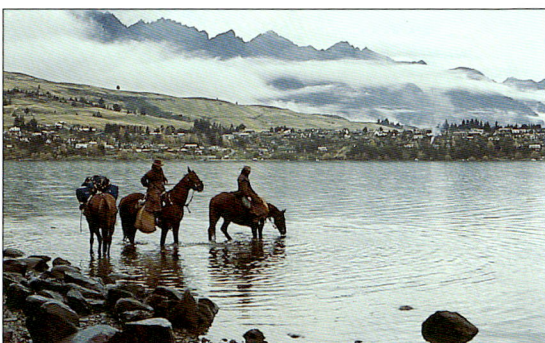
Lake Wakatipu

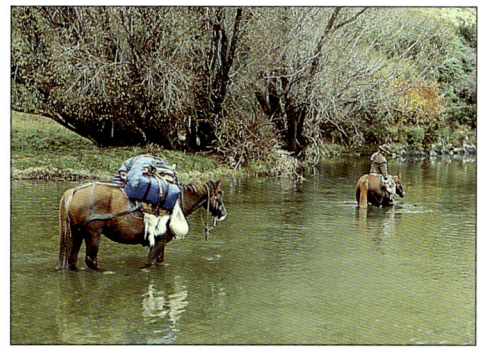
Crossing a river in Southland

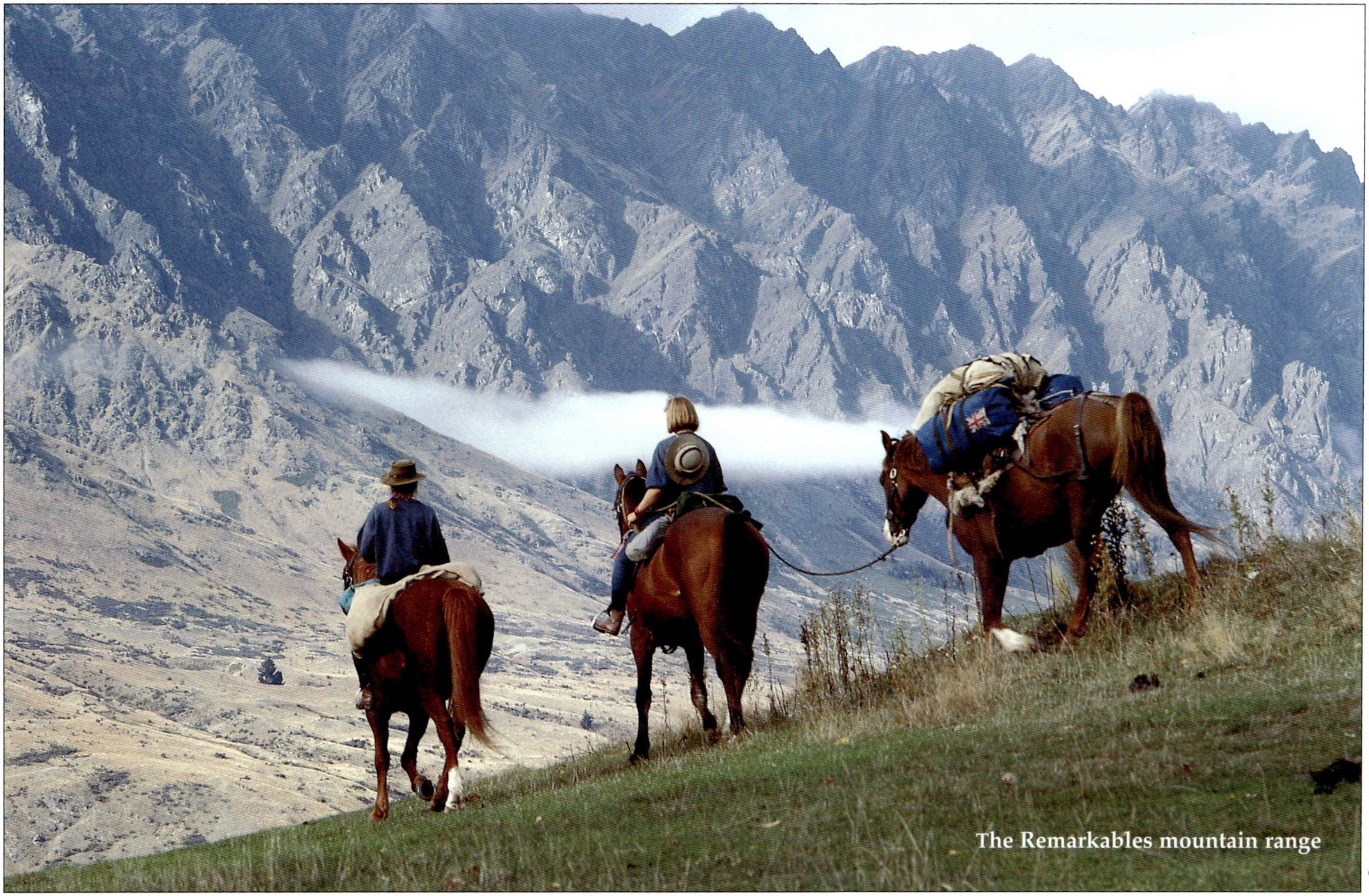

The Remarkables mountain range

Happy are those who trust in the Lord.
You have done many things for us, O Lord our God. There is none like You!
You have made many wonderful plans for us I could never speak of them all, their number is so great!
Psalm 40:5 GNB

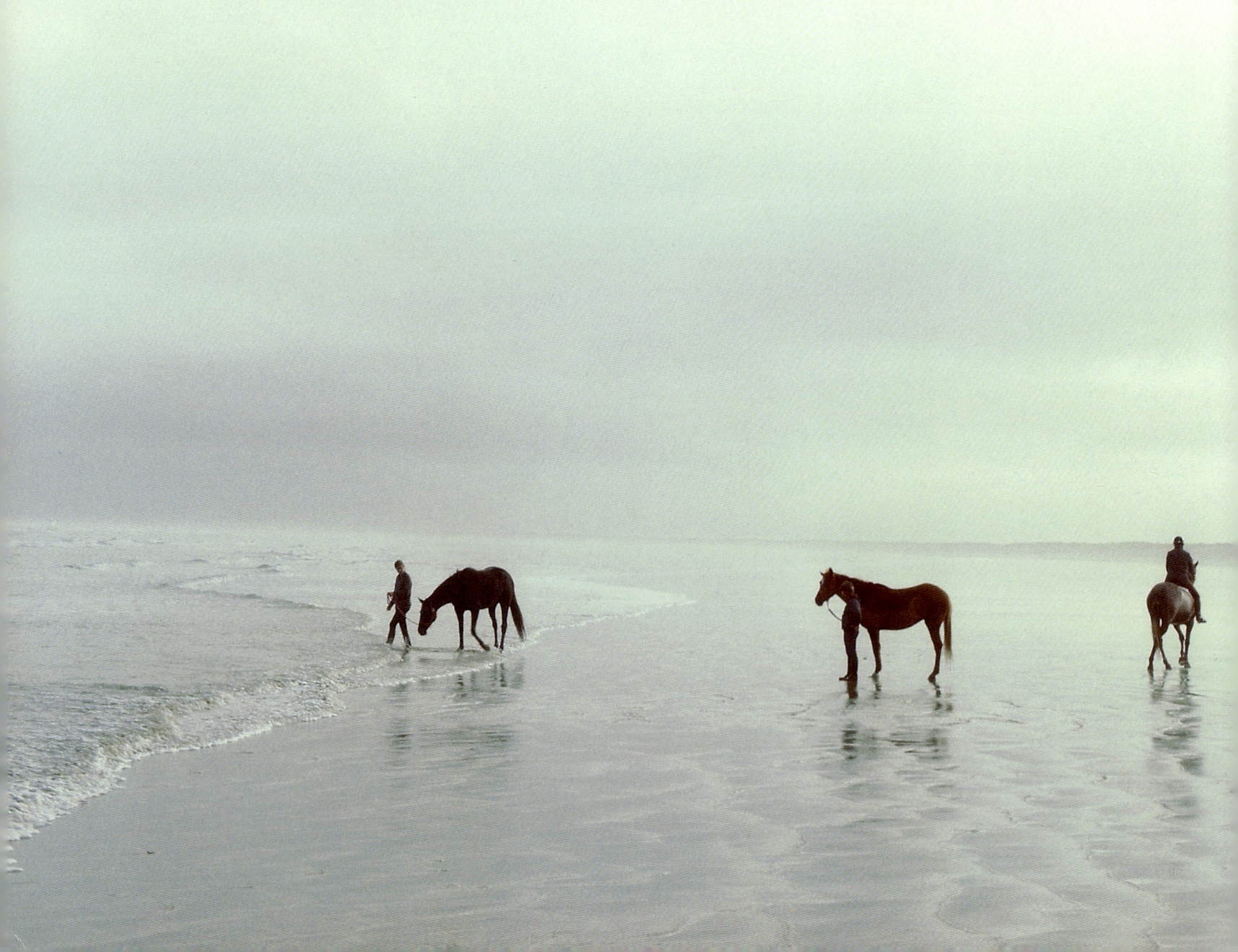

42

BLUFF

*Take delight in the Lord, and he will give you your heart's desires.
Commit everything you do to the Lord. Trust him, and he will help you.*
Psalm 37:4,5 NLT

The next morning I couldn't move. I was a mass of black-and-blue bruising colouring my body from my knees up to my chest. Gritting my teeth I rolled out of bed onto the floor but that was as far as I got that day! The following day I could shuffle to my horse and Ali gently gave me a leg-up into Nelson's saddle and we set out on our last stretch to the Bluff. The wind whipped up the sea into white capped horses and buffeted us from either side as we forged along an isthmus, towards the Bluff peninsula, under heavy hanging clouds.

We arrived at the bottom of New Zealand as the sun broke through the dark clouds and bathed us in its evening gold. Somehow the realisation that we had reached our destination was hard to take in as we sat under the Bluff signpost and our horses appreciatively munched their way through the carrots we held out to them.

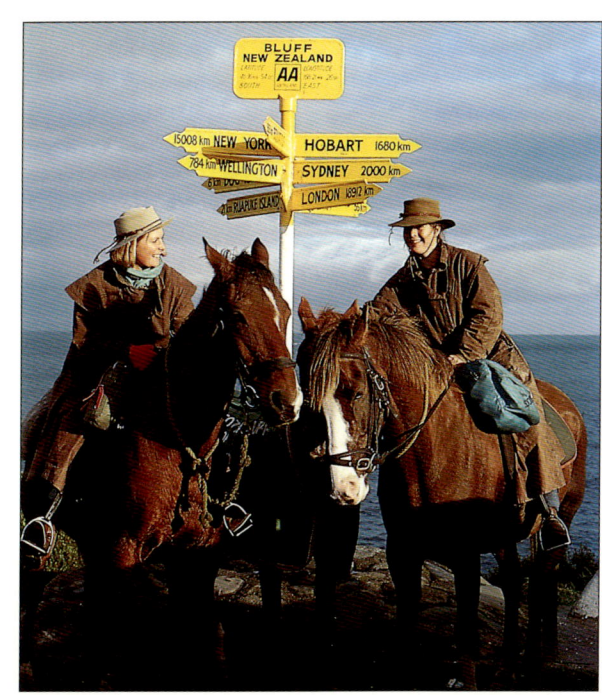

"Maybe we could just turn round and ride back up the country?" I suggested, as we didn't want our journey to end or to part with our horses.

"Then we would most definitely be outlaws on horseback!" Ali laughed and together we looked back on our last six months and recalled some of the many occasions of God's great faithfulness on our journey.

We had seen many times the New Zealand motto, *Take only photographs, leave only footprints.* I had taken lots of photographs and against all the odds we'd lived our dream and left two thousand miles of hoof prints the length of New Zealand.

On the South Coast

EPILOGUE

If it were not for becoming "Outlaws on horseback!" as our visas had almost expired for the third time, we would both have turned around and kept riding, so as to postpone having to part with our horses. We both found it heart-wrenching and however hard I tried, couldn't contain my tears at our parting.

It was snowing when we stood silently on the side of the road hitch-hiking north again. I felt a dreadful void not having our horses by our sides, I missed Monty's endearing face, and I even missed him demanding our attention, by barging through us and stepping on our toes!

With no option but to part with our horses, our greatest concern was to find them good homes. A seventy-three year old gentleman had bought Honey for long distance riding round the southern tip of New Zealand. They were a good match and could grow old together! Telling an older horse's age can be a bit uncertain and although we saved Honey from the meat-man as a thirteen year old, we reckoned she was probably a lot older! We gave our handsome leader Nelson to a lady who wanted a quiet hack, while Monty went off to become a dressage horse. From pack-horse to dressage horse! I could almost read his thoughts at our farewell,

"You see!" I saw the quizzical expression on his face,

"I was always destined to become something more than just a pack horse!"

"But Monty," I replied, stroking his nose affectionately as he rested his heavy muzzle endearingly on my shoulder, as was his habit "You were our very special pack-horse!"

But now, only their saddles lay at our feet being dusted in snow. I pondered on the many wonderful memories of our ride and the dream fulfilled.